Seeing With A Native Eye

P69 Chief Joseph surrender
80 vision quest
84
94 phenomenology

A HARPER FORUM BOOK

Edited by
Walter Holden Capps
Assisted by
Ernst F. Tonsing

Harper & Row, Publishers
New York
Hagerstown
San Francisco
London

Essays on
Native American
Religion

Seeing with a Native Eye

by

Åke Hultkrantz

Joseph Epes Brown

N. Scott Momaday

Sam D. Gill

Emory Sekaquaptewa

W. Richard Comstock

& Barre Toelken

SEEING WITH A NATIVE EYE. Copyright © 1976 by Walter Holden Capps. All rights reserved. Printed in the United States of America. No part of this book may be used or reproduced in any manner whatsoever without written permission except in the case of brief quotations embodied in critical articles and reviews. For information address Harper & Row, Publishers, Inc., 10 East 53rd Street, New York, N.Y. 10022. Published simultaneously in Canada by Fitzhenry & Whiteside Limited, Toronto.

FIRST EDITION

Designed by Dorothy Schmiderer

Library of Congress Cataloging in Publication Data

Main entry under title:
Seeing with a native eye.
  (A Harper forum book)
  Bibliography: p
  1. Indians of North America—Religion and
mythology—Addresses, essays, lectures.
I. Hultkrantz, Ake. II. Capps, Walter H.
E98.R3S37 1976   299'.7   76-9980
ISBN 0-06-061312 pbk.

76 77 78 79 10 9 8 7 6 5 4 3 2 1

Dedicated to Black Elk's vision
that there are spirit shapes of things
at the center of the world

Contents

Seeing With A Native Eye

Introduction

Seeing with a Native Eye consists of a series of glimpses into the religious horizon of native American peoples. Its proposal is straightforward—simply that native American religion needs to be reckoned with. This is its thesis, but it is also announcement and confession. It is announcement because it signals that a new area of scholarly inquiry has been opened. It is confession because, regrettably and tragically, the announcement has suffered long delay.

The thesis, the announcement, and the confession register in several different contexts. In terms of scholarship, for example, historians and philosophers of religion have come increasingly to realize the importance of native American religions. Professor Åke Hultkrantz of Stockholm University, a contributor to this volume, contends that no one can be properly trained in the study of religion unless he is well grounded in native American culture. This is an important contention. Yet one would hardly think that it need be made. After all, scholarly interest in the religions of native North Americans was expressed as early as the late nineteenth century. It was assisted indirectly by the research of such prominent American anthropologists as Franz Boas (1858–1942) and Paul Radin (1883–1959), the author of *The Autobiography of a Winnebago Indian* (1920).

From the perspective of the study of religion, however, it was an interest of a particular sort. It was supported primarily by an attempt to recover the origins of religion, from which one could then trace the evolution of religion. The Indians, the native North Americans, were the object of some scholarly intrigue under the expectation that they could give insights regarding these beginnings. The expectation was based on an assumption that the origins of religion may be

1

accessible via an analysis of the primitive mind. Native American culture was intriguing because it was understood to represent a way of apprehending reality that pertained prior to the onset of analytical forms of conceptualization. Religion was associated with *mythos*, as distinct from *logos*, and the native American was expected to help unlock the secrets of its primordial state.

But, as happens so frequently in the world of scholarship, the guiding hypothesis was called into question. Through the careful scrutiny of anthropologists like A. R. Radcliffe-Brown, E. E. Evans-Pritchard, and others, the assumptions underlying origin-and-development strategy were challenged. The origin of religion was deemed to be inaccessible, both methodologically and empirically, and additional difficulties were laid upon attempts to trace its evolution. As a result, scholarly interest in native American religion tended to diminish, and was replaced by other pursuits.

The new paradigm was influenced markedly by the contentions of Max Weber and Emile Durkheim. It purported to approach religion by deciphering the logic of tribal, social, and cultural organization. Instead of *origin*, *evolution*, and *development*, the language of the substitute interest was dotted with words like *sociocultural system, complex processes*, and organic coordination. The change in nomenclature indicated that interest had been shifted from first datum to the nature and composition of society. Religion itself was understood to be a component of society, always functioning in coordination and correspondence with other aspects.

There was good reason for the shift. The new interest carried conviction. It opened new worlds. It uncovered new facts. It made new realizations available. But in the shuffle, the interest in native American religion lost its original, sustaining intellectual rationale. Subsequently, it was accorded something less than a prominent scholarly place.

When interest in the subject was rekindled, and only very recently, it was not really because of subsequent shifts in patterns of inquiry and research. It was due more to the pervasive raising of consciousness that occurred in the 1960s and 1970s in American cultural life. It was stimulated by the temper of the social movements of the time, being included in a rebirth of emotional interest in recovering the fundamentals of human life. It was facilitated by the turn away from "establishment mores," together with the new sensitivity to the power of ethnicity, in addition to profound changes within native American communities themselves. And for many the guides into the new adventure lands were writers like John Neihardt, author of *Black Elk Speaks*, Joseph Epes Brown, author of *The Sacred Pipe*, Frank Waters, and, perhaps preeminently, Carlos Castaneda, with his account of the teachings of Don Juan. These are writers familiar with the folkways and attitudes of native Americans. They portrayed these in images and language that fascinated outsiders.

This is the other context for the announcement and the confession. We refer to the tragically belated recognition of the profound character of native American religions. Now, little more than a half century following the massacre at Wounded Knee, and less than a century following the death of such large heroic figures as Chief Joseph of the Nez Perce, the nonnative American is coming to an awareness that native Americans possess attitudes and perspectives that have a significant appeal. There is a growing recognition that native Americans should be taken seriously, and not simply in principle. More and more, nonnative Americans are attracted to native American cultural and religious traditions. They look to these as sources of insight, assistance, sustenance, and transformation.

The turnabout reflects transitions and crises in nonnative American social and cultural life. Increasingly, the prevailing value schemes of majority America have come under challenge because of failures, disappointments, and frustrations. When the use and misuse of the environment makes the air too choked to breathe and the water too foul to drink, when ecology is out of balance, when energy is dissipated, when the artifacts of civilization threaten to destroy both man and civilization, then it seems appropriate to try to penetrate through the world of fabricated material culture to some basis of elemental harmony in humanity's relation to that which ulimately sustains us. We are suggesting that the nonnative American is turning to the native American to teach us effectively to cope with illusion. Coupled with this deep-seated interest in rediscovering the fundamentals is a newly found insistence that human life become more simplified. We mean simple in the sense of single, not as being simplistic. The intertwined lines of organic coordination have become too numerous, too tangled, and too mentally, spiritually, and emotionally taxing. Twentieth-century men and women feel overextended, conflicted, misaligned, and even tricked at times. Thus, there is profound disenchantment, and an earnestness to recover primordial origins. This recovery holds the prospect of restoring humanity's correct alignment with the universe and reconstituting our sense of identity.

The astounding fact is that native Americans tend to welcome this turnabout. The reason may be not only the admission of previous injustices which it implies. A larger factor is the revolution in self-consciousness which native Americans are also experiencing. They have seized the new openness as an occasion for coming to terms with their own emerging self-identity. They do not want to be what they once were, or were portrayed to be, in some previous historical or "prehistorical" era. But the people want to become what they are today, in the mid-twentieth century, in a world in which technology, bureaucracies, large institutions, and various sorts of political and economic nationalisms tend to rule.

There is a new openness on both sides. And in many places the native American is involved in a kind of "dialogue" with the nonnative American which both welcome for their own purposes. Even in the newer climate, the offense and testiness remain present. The memory of the past is too fresh, and the nature of the relationship too fragile to offset the fears that exploitation will continue. It does continue. The grievances—the violence, the massacres, the widespread tribal genocide—have not been redressed. The price of wrongdoing has not been paid, nor could it ever be. And the exploitation continues. Whereas the white man formerly took the Indian's lands and goods, now we take their ideas—when it suits us or when we have need of them. In all such transactions, there is no true medium of exchange. Yet, because the new era has occurred at precisely the same time that native Americans are becoming more astute politically regarding their corporate needs, there is a sense of urgency, and some hints of optimism, in the conversations taking place. As Joseph Epes Brown indicates in remarks included in this volume, both traditions—both Anglo and native American—are currently involved in a "quest for the roots of lost heritages." To a certain extent, both traditions have found that they can be engaged in the same quest together.

Somehing of this temper is reflected in the chapters following. Barre Toelken, of the University of Oregon, approaches the subject in the very title of his paper "Seeing with a Native Eye," which we have also adopted as the title of this book. Toelken's deceptively simple account is an eloquent attempt to assist the nonnative American to see what native Americans see. He is interested in identifying various or alternative patterns of perception, and he wants to chart the influence of these various perception patterns upon the formation of concepts and ideas within selected cultures. It is no secret that Toelken's viewpoint has been informed by the writings of Benjamin Whorf and Edward T. Hall, the latter the author of *The Hidden Dimension* and *The Silent Language*.

A similar theme is pursued in Joseph Epes Brown's essay. Currently on the faculty of the University of Montana, and the dean among American scholars in this field, Brown tries to provide accessibility to the worldview of the native American in terms the nonnative American can at least approach. He proceeds by cataloguing and describing some of the key themes and categories, as though he were engaged in preliminary phenomenological investigation, of native-American sensitivity.

Emory Sekaquaptewa, a member of the Hopi tribe and a professor in the University of Arizona, selects an example from his own culture to draw the nonnative American into an unfamiliar way of life and assist him in coming to terms with it. For Sekaquaptewa, this role is assigned to the kachina doll. He analyzes the kachina ceremony to illustrate prominent attitudes and aspirations of the Hopi people, contending that the kachina doll becomes the form of security for the child, symbolizing harmony between individual, community, and nature.

Sam Gill of Arizona State University explores in a similar manner. Taking a rather ordinary experience, a meeting between two Navajo families, Gill proceeds to demonstrate its deeper significance. He finds the event to reflect the fundamental disposition through which native American peoples apprehend reality.

W. Richard Comstock of the University of California, Santa Barbara, turns the subject in the other direction. Instead of attempting to recreate the horizon of native Americans in terms perspicuous to nonnative Americans, Comstock recounts a number of significant portrayals of native Americans by "native Europeans." Using cinema as his principle medium, Comstock also chronicles a distinctive recent shift in imagery drawn upon for this purpose.

The nature theme predominates in N. Scott Momaday's essay. Momaday's intention is to illustrate native American sensitivity to nature, the land, and the earth. As a Kiowa Indian, who spent his childhood on reservations in the Southwest, Momaday knows the subject firsthand. As a Pulitzer-Prize–winning novelist, he is also well able to express this feeling.

The most comprehensive essay in the collection is provided by Åke Hultkrantz, who is generally regarded as the foremost authority on this subject among scholars in religious studies. Being personally responsible for stimulating interest in the subject among a large group of students and colleagues, Hultkrantz describes the state of the field to date. Next, he maps out the methodological and substantive tasks that must also be tackled. It is clear that he views the subject as being far from peripheral importance. For Hultkrantz, the study of native American religions and cultures reaches the very core of religious studies itself.

The two prominent contemporary stimuli—the crisis in American values, and the new recognition of the scholarly importance of the subject—are identified, discussed, and interrelated in the edited panel discussion which forms the final chapter of the book. Originally, the panel discussion occurred on a television program as part of a symposium on native American religions sponsored by the Institute of Religious Studies of the University of California, Santa Barbara. Careful readers will recognize that the panel discussion remains unfinished. Video-taping time ran out before the discussion could be completed. Before this occurred, the participants came to agree that native American religions, because of their obvious significance, ought to be included in comparative and phenomenological studies in religion. But they also recognized that such studies do not always produce an understanding of such religions that would be shared by the native American. Had there been more time, the participants in the symposium might have drawn up detailed recommendations regarding future work, curriculum development, research areas, means of disseminating information to the public schools, etc. Yet, it is also strong testimony to the power of the subject matter and to the compulsions it generates that there was resistance to discussions of such practical matters. Perhaps we recognized that proceeding further in this area, whether directly or indirectly, would involve us in the repetition of the same (though more subtle) form of exploitation that had been occurring right along. To engage in such efforts would eventually require that we subject a unique and intrinsic cultural heritage to alien forms of expression and utility. And this, in turn, would simply keep the tired, stultifying, and discordant pattern alive. Whatever is inserted into a particular complex of meaning—even if it is simply a curricular design—tends to pull both form and content from the context in which it is placed. We considered taking the additional step, then held back, hoping that our action might persuade the vision— "seeing with a native eye"—to abide a bit longer. Practical curricular matters must be faced evenually. Indeed, the symposium participants want to encourage the same. But the power of the imagery made us content to leave the subsequent agenda for a later time.

Before giving way to the essays themselves, I want to record thanks to the distinguished participants in the symposium, and to my colleagues and the students of the University of California, Santa Barbara. Martha Oppenheim, Tina Keene, and Deborah Sills performed the necessary transcription and typing tasks. Several scholars, both at home and abroad, read and criticized previous versions of the manuscript. For this all of us are grateful. Special thanks also are due to Professor Toelken for his willingness to allow a portion of the title of his paper to stand as the title of the book. Deep thanks are due to Professor E. Fred Tonsing, now of California Lutheran College, who helped organize the symposium, assisting enormously in its execution as well as in the preparation of the manuscript.

WALTER H. CAPPS

Santa Barbara, California
March 23, 1976

Seeing with a Native Eye:
How Many Sheep Will It Hold?

BARRE TOELKEN

There are some things that one knows already if he or she has read very much about the native Americans. One of the most important is that there is almost nothing that can be said about "the Indians" as a whole. Every tribe is different from every other in some respects, and similar in other respects, so that nearly everything one says normally has to be qualified by footnotes. What I am about to say here does not admit room for that. I propose, therefore, to give a few examples from the Navajo culture and make some small glances at other Indian cultures that I know a little bit about; that is simply a device to keep my observations from appearing as though they were meant to be generally applicable to Indians of the whole country.

It is estimated that there were up to 2,000 separate cultures in the Northern hemisphere before the advent of the white man. Many of these groups spoke mutually unintelligible languages. Anthropologists estimate that there were as many as eighty such languages in the Pacific Northwest alone. In terms of language and traditions, these cultures were very much separated from each other; and although they have been lumped into one category by whites ever since (and that is the source of some of our problems), any given Indian will have a few things in common with some other tribes and many things not in common with others. My generalizations are made with this in mind from the start. But one must start *somewhere* in an attempt to cope with the vast conceptual gulf which lies between Anglos in general and natives in general, for it is a chasm which has not often been bridged, especially in religious discussion.

I do not claim, either, to be one of those rare people who *have* succeeded in making the leap—an insider, a confidant, a friend of the Red Man's Council Fire—in short, one of those Tarzans even more rare in reality than one would conclude from their memoirs. But I did have the good fortune to be adopted by an old Navajo, Tsinaabąąs Yazhi ("Little Wagon"), in southern Utah in the mid-fifties during the uranium rush. I moved in with his family, learned Navajo, and lived essentially a Navajo life for roughly two years. Of course I have gone back since then on every possible occasion to visit my family, although my adopted father is now dead, as is his wife and probably 50 percent of the people I knew in the fifties. If one has read the Navajo statistics he knows why. This is not intended to be a tale of woe, however; I simply want it understood that I was not a missionary among the Navajo. Nor was I an anthropologist, a teacher, a tourist, or any of the other things that sometimes cause people to come to know another group briefly and superficially. Although, indeed, at one time I had it in my mind to stay with them forever, it is probably because my culture did not train me to cope with almost daily confrontation with death that I was unable to do so. I learned much from them, and it is no exaggeration to say that a good part of my education was gained there. It was probably the most important part. "Culture shock" attended my return to the Anglo world even though I left the Navajos as "un-Navajo" as when I arrived.

With that for background, though, I think I can say something about how differently we see things, envision things, look at things, how dissimilarly different cultures try to process the world of reality, which, for many native American tribes, includes the world of religion. In Western culture, religion seems to occupy a niche reserved for the unreal, the Otherworld, a reference point that is reached only upon death or through the agency of the priest. Many native American tribes see religious experience as something that surrounds man all the time. In fact, my friends the Navajos would say that there is probably *nothing* that can be called nonreligious. To them, almost anything anyone is likely to do has some sort of religious significance, and many other tribes concur. Procedurally, then, our problem is how to learn to talk about religion, even in preliminary ways, knowing perfectly well that in one society what is considered art may in another be considered religion, or that what is considered as health in one culture may be religion in another. Before we can proceed, in other words, we need to reexamine our categories, our "pigeonholes," in order to "see" things through someone else's set of patterns. This is the reason for the odd title: "Seeing with a Native Eye."

Through our study of linguistics and anthropology we have learned that different groups of people not only think in different ways, but that they often "see" things in different ways. Good scientific experiments can be provided, for example, to prove that if certain ideas are offered to people in patterns which they have not been taught to recognize, not only will they not understand them, they often will not even see them. We see things in "programmed" ways. Of course Professor Whorf was interested in demonstrating the pervasiveness of this theory with respect to language, and many anthropologists and linguists have had reservations about his theories. But the experimentation continues, and there is some interesting and strong evidence that a person will look right through something that he or she is not trained to see, and that different cultures train people in different ways. I will not get into the Jungian possibilities that we may be born with particularized codes as well; this is beyond my area of expertise. But it is clear that when we want to talk about native American religion, we want to try to see it as much as possible (if it is possible) with the "native eye". That is to say, if we talk about native American religions using the categories of Western religions, we are simply going to see what *we* already know is there. We will recognize certain kinds of experiences as religious, and we will cancel out others. To us, for example, dance may be an art form, or it may be a certain kind of kinesis. With certain native American tribes, dance may be the most religious act a person can perform. These differences are very significant; on the basis of this kind of cultural blindness, for example, Kluckhohn classified the Navajo coyote tales as "secular" primarily because they are humorous.

The subtitle of this paper comes from my adopted Navajo father. My first significant educational experience came when I was trying to educate him to what the outside world looked like. Here was an eighty- or ninety-year-old man in the 1950s who had never seen a paved road or a train; he had seen airplanes flying overhead and was afraid of them. He had seen almost nothing of what you and I experience as the "modern, advanced world." I decided I would try to cushion the shock for him by showing him pictures, and then I would invite him into town with me sometime when I went to Salt Lake City. I felt he needed some preparation for the kind of bombardment of the senses one experiences in the city after living out in the desert.

I showed him a two-page spread of the Empire State Building which appeared in *Life* that year. His question was, immediately, "How many sheep will it hold?" I had to admit that I didn't know, and that even if I did know, I couldn't count that high in Navajo; and I tried to show him how big a sheep might look if you held it up against one of those windows, but he was interested neither in my excuses nor in my intent to explain the size of the building. When I told him what it was for, he was shocked. The whole concept of so many people filed together in one big drawer—of course he would not have used those terms—was shocking to him. He felt that people who live so close together cannot live a very rich life, so he expected that whites would be found to be spiritually impoverished and personally very upset by living so close together. I tried to assure him that this was not so. Of course I was wrong. Little by little one learns.

The next episode in this stage of my learning occurred about six months later, when I was at the trading post and found a magazine with a picture of the latest jet bomber on it. I brought that to him to explain better what those things were that flew over all the time. He asked the same question in spite of the fact there were lots of little men standing around the plane and he could see very well how big it was. Again he said, "How many sheep will it carry?" I started to shrug him off as if he were simply plaguing me, when it became clear to me that what he was really asking was, "What is it good for in terms of something that I know to be valid and viable in the world?" (That, of course, is not his wording either.) In effect, he was saying that he was not willing even to try to understand the Empire State Building or the bomber unless I could give those particular sensations to him in some kind of patternings from which he could make some assessment. He was not really interested in how big they were, he was interested in what they were doing in the world. When I told him what the jet bomber was for, he became so outraged that he refused ever to go to town, and he died without ever having done so as far as I know. He said that he had heard many terrible things about the whites, but the idea of someone killing that many people by dropping the bomb and remaining so far out of reach that he was not in danger was just too much!

The only other thing that approached such outrage, by the way, was when I explained to him about the toilet facilities in white houses, and I mentioned indoor toilet functions. He could hardly believe that one. "They do that right in the house, right inside where everyone lives?" "No, no, you don't understand. There is a separate room for it." That was even worse—that there could be a special place for such things. A world so neatly categorized and put in boxes really bothered him, and he steadfastly refused to go visit it. At the time I thought he was being what we call primitive, backward—he was dragging his feet, refusing to understand the march of science and culture. What I "see" now is that, as a whole, he was simply unable to—it did not "compute" in the way we might put it today; he did not "see" what I meant. In turn, he was trying to call my attention to that fact, and I was not receiving the impression.

I bring these matters up not because they are warm reminiscences, but because difficulties in communicating religious ideas are parallel to these examples. When my adopted father asked, "How many sheep will it hold?" he was asking, "What is it doing here, how does it function? Where does it go? Why do such things occur in the world?" We might consider the Pueblo view that in the spring-time Mother Earth is pregnant, and one does not mistreat her any more than one might mistreat a pregnant woman. When our technologists go and try to get Pueblo farmers to use steel plows in the spring, they are usually rebuffed. For us it is a technical idea—"Why don't you just use plows? You plow, and you get 'x' results from doing so." For the Pueblos this is meddling with a formal religious idea (in Edward Hall's terms). Using a plow, to borrow the Navajo phrase, "doesn't hold any sheep." In other words, it does not make sense in the way in which the world operates. It is against the way things really go. Some Pueblo folks still take the heels off their shoes, and sometimes the shoes off their horses, during the spring. I once asked a Hopi whom I met in that country, "Do you mean to say, then, that if I kick the ground with my foot, it will botch everything up, so nothing will grow?" He said, "Well, I don't know whether that would happen or not, but it would just really show what kind of person you are."

One learns slowly that in many of these native religions, religion is viewed as embodying the reciprocal relationships between people and the sacred *processes* going on in the world. It may not involve a "god." It may not be signified by praying or asking for favors, or doing what may "look" religious to people in our culture. For the Navajo, for example, almost *everything* is related to health. For us health is a medical issue. We may have a few home remedies, but for most big things we go to a doctor. A Navajo goes to the equivalent of a priest to get well because one needs not only medicine, the Navajo would say, but one needs to reestablish his relationship with the rhythms of nature. It is the ritual as well as the medicine which gets one back "in shape." The medicine may cure the symptoms, but it won't cure you. It does not put you back in step with the things, back in the natural cycles—this is a job for the "singer." Considering the strong psychological and spiritual role of such a person, it should not come as a surprise that it is on spiritual (magic?) grounds, not medicinal, that some medicinal materials are *not* used. For example, Pete Catches, a Sioux medicine man (who practices the Eagle "way" of the Sacred Pipe), knows about but will not employ abortion-producing plants, for such use would run counter to and thus impede the ritualistic function of the pipe ceremony, a good part of which is to help increase the live things in the world. In the reciprocative life pattern, death is not a proper ingredient.

I want to go a little further into this, because these patterns, these cycles, these reciprocations that we find so prominently in native American religions, are things which for our culture are not only puzzling but often considered absolutely insane. It is the conflict or incongruency in patterning that often impedes our understanding. Let me give a few examples of this patterning. In Western culture —I suppose in most of the technological cultures—there has been a tremendous stress on lineal patterning and lineal measurements, grid patterns, straight lines. I think one reason for this is that technological cultures have felt that it is not only desirable but even necessary to control nature. We know there are very few straight lines in nature. One of the ways people can tell if they are controlling nature is to see that it is put in straight lines—we have to put things "in order." And so we not only put our filing cases and our books in straight lines and alphabetical "order", we also put nature in straight lines and grid patterns—our streets, our houses, our acreage, our lives, our measurement of time and space, our preference for the shortest distance between two points, our extreme interest in being "on time."

Those who have read the works of Hall and other anthropologists on the anthropology of time and space are familiar with these ideas. Each culture has a kind of spatial system through which one knows by what he sees as he grows up how close he can stand to someone else, how he is to walk in public and in private, where his feet are supposed to fall, where things are supposed to go. These patterns show up in verbal expressions too—we have to "get things straightened out," "get things straight between us," make someone "toe the line." We also arrange classrooms and auditoriums in some sort of lineal order (other groups might want these to be arranged in a circle). To us, having things "in order" means lining things up, getting things in line. We talk about "getting straight with one another," looking straight into each other's eyes, being "straight shooters." We even talk about the "straight" people vs. the "groovy" people. Notice how we often depict someone who is crazy with a circular hand motion around the ear. Someone who does not speak clearly "talks in circles," or uses circuitous logic. We think of logic itself as being in straight lines: A plus B equals C. We look forward to the conclusion of things, we plan into the future, as though time were a sort of straight track along which we move toward certain predictable goals.

If one knows much about native Americans of almost any tribe, he realizes that I am choosing, intentionally, certain lineal and grid patterns which are virtually unmatched in native American patterns. We learn to find each other in the house or in the city by learning the intersection of straight lines—so many doors down the hallway is the kitchen, or the bathroom, and we are never to confuse them. We separate them. One does not cook in the bathroom—it is ludicrous to get them mixed up. We have it all neatly separated and categorized. For most native American groups, almost the reverse is true—things are brought together. Instead of separating into categories of this sort, family groups sit in circles, meetings are in circles, dances are often—not always—in circles, especially the dances intended to welcome and include people. With the exception of a few tribes such as the Pueblo peoples, who live in villages which have many straight lines, most of the tribes usually live (or lived) in round dwellings like the hogan of the Navajo, the tipi of the plains Indians, the igloo of the Eskimo. The Eastern Indians and some Northwestern tribes sometimes lived in long houses, but the families or clans sat in circles within.

There is, then, a "logical" tendency to recreate the pattern of the circle at every level of the culture, in religion as well as in social intercourse. I think the reason for it is that what makes sense, what "holds sheeep" for many tribes, is the concept that reciprocation is at the heart of everything going on in the world. I have had Pueblo people tell me that what they are doing when they participate in rain dances or fertility dances is not asking help from the sky; rather, they are doing something which they characterize as a hemisphere which is brought together in conjunction with another hemisphere. It is a participation in a kind of interaction which I can only characterize as sacred reciprocation. It is a sense that everything always goes this way. We are always interacting, and if we refuse to interact, or if some taboo action has caused a break in this interaction, then disease or calamity comes about. It is assumed that reciprocation is the order of things, and so we will expect it to keep appearing in all forms.

I think that it makes anthropological and linguistic sense to say that any culture will represent things religiously, artistically, and otherwise, the way its members "see" things operating in the world. But here is where the trick comes in. When we from one culture start looking at the patterns of another culture, we will often see what *our* culture has trained us to see. If we look at a Navajo rug, for example, we are inclined to say that Navajos use many straight lines in their rugs. And yet if we talk to Navajos about weaving, the *gesture* we often see is a four-way back-and-forth movement; and they talk about the interaction within the pattern—a reciprocation. Most often the Navajo rug reciprocates its pattern from side to side and from end to end, creating mirror images. My adopted sister, who is a very fine weaver, always talks about this kind of balance. She says, "When I am thinking up these patterns, I am trying to spin something, and then I unspin it. It goes up this way and it comes down that way." And she uses circular hand gestures to illustrate. While we are trained to see the straight lines, and to think of the rug in terms of geometric patterns, she makes the geometrical necessities of weaving—up one, over one—fit a kind of circular logic about how nature works and about how man interacts with nature. If we are going to talk about her beliefs with respect to rugs, we need somehow to project ourselves into her circles.

Let me give a couple of other examples. These, by the way, are not intended to be representative, but are just some things that I have encountered. They are simply illustrative of the way a Navajo might explain things. There is a species of beads that one often finds in curio shops these days. They are called "ghost" beads by the whites, though I do not know any Navajos who call them that except when talking to whites (they feel they ought to phrase it the way the whites will undersand it). The brown beads in these arrangements are the inside of the blue juniper berries, which the Navajo call literally "juniper's eyes." In the most preferred way of producing these necklaces, Navajos search to find where the small ground animals have hidden their supply of juniper seeds. Usually a small girl, sometimes a boy, will look for likely hiding places, scoop them all out when she find them, and look for the seeds that have already been broken open, so as not to deprive the animals of food. She puts all the whole seeds back, and takes only the ones that have a hole in one end. She takes them home, cleans them, punches a hole in the other end with a needle, and strings them together. I do not know any Navajo in my family or among my acquaintances who ever goes without these beads on him some-where, usually in his pocket.

My Navajo sister says that reason these beads will prevent night-mares and keep one from getting lost in the dark is that they represent the partnership between the tree that gives its berries, the animals which gather them, and humans who pick them up (being careful not to deprive the animals of their food). It is a three-way partnership—plant, animal, and man. Thus, if you keep these beads on you and think about them, your mind, in its balance with nature, will tend to lead a healthy existence. If you are healthy by Navajo standards, you are participating properly in all the cycles of nature, and thus you will not have bad dreams. Bad dreams are a *sign* of being sick, and getting lost is a *sign* of being sick. So these beads are not for warding off sickness itself; rather, they are reminders of a frame of mind which is essentially cyclic, in the proper relationship with the rest of nature—a frame of mind necessary to the maintenance of health.

Again, using the weaving of rugs as an example, I want to explain the significance of the spindle and the yarn. The yarn comes from the sheep, of course. The Navajos explain the relationship there not in terms of the rug, the end product—which, of course, is what our culture is interested in—but in terms of the relationship with the yarn and with the sheep, and with the spinning of the yarn, which has to be done in a certain direction because it goes along with everything else that is spinning. Everything for the Navajos is moving; an arbitrary term in English such as *east* is phrased in Navajo, "something round moves up regularly." When one spins the yarn, then, one does not just twist it to make string out of it; one twists it in the right direction (sunwise) with everything else (otherwise, the thread will ravel). Thus, the yarn itself becomes a further symbol of man's interaction with the animal on the one hand, and with the whole of the cosmos on the other. When one works with yarn one is working with something that remains a symbol of the cyclic or circular interaction with nature. Even the spindle can be seen as an agency of, or a focal point in, a religious view of man and nature.

In a recent experiment by an anthropologist and a moviemaker, some young Navajos were given cameras and encouraged to make their own movies. One girl made a movie called "Navajo Weaving." It lasts, as I recall, almost forty-five minutes, but there are only a few pictures of rugs in it. Most of the film is about people riding horseback, wandering out through the sagebrush, feeding the sheep, sometimes shearing them, sometimes following them through the desert, sometimes picking and digging the roots from which the dyes are made. Almost the entire film is made up of the things that the Navajo find important about making rugs: human interaction with nature. That is what rugmaking is for the Navajos. Something which for us is a secular craft or a technique is for these people a part or extension of the reciprocations embodied in religion.

Religious reciprocity extends even into the creation of the rug's design. My Navajo sister wove a rug for me as a gift, the kind which the traders call *yei* (*yei* means something like "the holy people"). The pattern in this particular rug is supposed to represent five lizard people. The two on opposite ends are the same color, and the next two inward the same color, and the one in the middle a distinctly different color. The middle one is the dividing line, so that the pattern reciprocates from end to end of the rug. When my sister gave it to me, she said, "These represent your five children." Of course I was moved to inquire of her why she should represent my five children as lizards (I had private ideas about why she might). I wondered what her reasoning was, and I certainly knew children are not "holy people"—far from it. She pointed out, "Your oldest and youngest are girls, and they are represented by the two opposite figures on each end. Then you have twin boys—they are the two white ones, because they are alike. Then there is another boy, who doesn't have a mate in your family, so he is the center point of the family, even though he isn't that in terms of age." She made the pattern reciprocate from one end to the other not only in terms of representing my family but in terms of color. All the dyes were from particular plants which were related in her mind to good health. Lizards represent longevity, and by making my children congruent with the lizard people, she was making a statement of, an embodiment of, their health and longevity. This is a wish that any Navajo might want to express, because, as noted above, health and longevity are central to Navajo religious concerns.

If I knew more about the symbolic function of certain colors in the rug, or the use of the dye-producing plants in Navajo medicine, I have no doubt that I would have still more to say about the religious expression intended therein.

Reciprocity is central to the production of many other Navajo items, especially so in the making of moccasins. My brother-in-law, Yellowman, when he goes hunting for skins to put on the body, tries to produce what the Navajos call "sacred deerskin." It is supposed to be produced from a deer whose hide is not punctured in the killing. If one wants the deer for meat, it can be simply shot (Yellowman, though he is in his early sixties, still hunts with a bow and arrow). But when he hunts deer for moccasins, or for cradle boards for his family (the deerskin helps to surround the baby), then he wants skin of the sacred kind. To obtain sacred deerskin in the old fashion, one runs the deer down until it is exhausted, and then smothers it to death.

It is done in this manner: one first gathers pollen, which he carries with him in a small pouch. He then gets the deer out into open country and jogs along behind it, following until it is totally exhausted. Deer run very rapidly for awhile but soon get tired. The man who is good at jogging can keep it up for some distance. Still, it is no easy job, as you can imagine if you have ever visited the desert of the Monument Valley area. When the deer is finally caught, he is thrown to the ground as gently as possible, his mouth and nose are held shut, and covered with a handful of pollen so that he may die breathing the sacred substance. And then—I am not sure how widespread this is with the Navajos—one sings to the deer as it is dying, and apologizes ritually for taking its life, explaining that he needs the skin for his family. The animal is skinned in a ritual way, and the rest of the deer is disposed of in a ritual manner (I do not feel free to divulge the particulars here).

The deerhide is brought home and tanned in the traditional way. The coloration is taken from particular kinds of herbs and from parts of the deer (including its brains). Then the moccasins are made by sewing the deerhide uppers together with cowhide soles.

In many cases they are buried in wet sand until the person for whom they are designed comes by. He puts them on and wears them until they are dry. In so doing, of course, he wears his footprints into them. You can always tell when you have on someone else's moccasins, if that mistake should ever occur, because they hurt. Your own toe prints are in your own moccasins, for they have become part of you. It is no accident that the word for moccasin or shoe is *shi ke*', "my shoe," which is exactly the same word for "my foot." Religiously speaking, what happens is that the deerskin becomes part of us, and this puts us in an interactive relationship with the deer. The whole event is ritualized, carried out in "proper" ways, because it falls into a formal religious category, not a mere craft. The moccasin is more than something to keep the foot warm and dry: it is symbolic of that sacred relation and interaction with the plants and the animals that the Navajo see as so central to "reality."

Also central to Navajo religion is the restoration of health when it has been lost. The *hogan* is the round dwelling the Navajos live in. The fire is in the middle of the floor, and the door always faces east. One of the reasons for this, as my adopted father told me, was to make sure that people always live properly oriented to the world of nature. The door frames the rising sun at a certain time of the year. The only light that comes in is either through the smokehole on the top, or through the door, if it happens to be open. Healing rituals involving "sandpainting" are usually enacted inside the hogan, and are oriented to the four directions. When the patient takes his or her place on the sandpainting, ritually they are taking their place within the world of the "holy people," related to all the cycling and reciprocation of the universe. It is partly that orientation which cures one.

Yellowman still hunts for meat with bow and arrow. His arrowheads are made out of ordinary carpenters' nails pounded out between rocks, although he has a whole deerskin bag of stone arrowheads that he has picked up on the desert. When I asked him why he did not use those nice stone points on his own arrows, he looked at me very strangely. (I knew that the Navajos put them in the bottom of medicine containers when they are making medicine, but I thought that perhaps he knew how to make them himself given the proper kind of rock.) I asked whether he knew how the old-timers used to make them. He looked at me as if I were absolutely insane. He finally answered, "Men don't make them at all; lizards make arrowheads." For him, stone arrowheads, such as one might find, are sacred items, and they fall into the same category as lizards, lightning, and corn pollen. Lizards, as I mentioned earlier, are related to long life and good health. When one finds a lizard or an arrowhead, he picks it up and holds it against the side of his arm or over his heart, the same places where pollen is placed during a ceremony. Clearly, stone arrowheads are for curing, not killing; or, more properly, they are for killing *diseases*. Thus, even arrowheads have to do with special sacred medicinal categories, not with the kinds of practical categories our culture might see. In other words, learning about Navajo religion and daily life requires the learning of a whole new set of concepts, codes, patterns, and assumptions.

A student of mine paraphrased an old proverb this way: "If I hadn't believed it I never would have seen it." This is essentially what I am saying about viewing religion in other cultures. Our usual approach is in terms of pictures, patterns, gestures, and attitudes that we already know how to see. For example, when some dance specialists went to Tucson a couple of years ago to watch the Yaqui Easter ceremonies, all they saw were the dances. They did not see that on a couple of occasions, several people very prominent in the ritual were simply sitting next to the altar for extremely long periods of time. I talked to almost every person at that conference, and only a few of them had seen those people sitting there. There wasn't any dancing going on there, and so the dance people weren't "seeing." And yet it was probably a very important part of the dance. I do not pretend to have understood this part, but the point is that the strangers had not even seen it; they were watching for what they as Anglos and dance specialists could recognize as dance steps. I would not accuse them of stupidity, ignorance, or narrowmindedness. Rather, they had not been taught to "read," to see other kinds of patternings than their own.

To complicate matters further, many tribes feel the real world is not one that is most easily seen, while the Western technological culture thinks of *this* as the real world, the one that *can* be seen and touched easily. To many native Americans the world that is real is the one we reach through special, religious means, the one we are taught to "see" and experience *via* ritual and sacred patterning. Instead of demanding proof for the Otherworld, as the scientific mind does, many native Americans are likely to counter by demanding proof that *this* one exists in any real way, since, by itself, it is not ritualized.

What the different cultures are taught to see, and how they see it, are thus worlds apart (although not, I think, mutually exclusive). One culture looks for a meaning in the visible, one looks for a meaning beyond the visible. The "cues" are different because the referents and the connotations are different. Add to this basic incongruency the fact that the patterning of one is based on planning, manipulation, predictability, competition, and power, while the other is based in reciprocation, "flowering," response to situation, and cooperation— and who would be surprised to find that the actual symbols and meanings of the two religious modes will be perceived and expressed in quite contrastive forms? We must seek to understand the metaphor of the native American, and we must be willing to witness to the validity of its sacred function, or else we should not pretend to be discussing this religion. Before we can see, we must learn how to look.

2

The Roots of Renewal

JOSEPH EPES BROWN

There is an unprecedented explosion of interest today in all facets of the native American heritage. It is especially significant that this interest and concern are shared by the native American and the nonnative American alike. Analyses of the complex reasons for this concern is outside the scope of this paper. But it may be suggested that behind it all lies the native American's increasing dis-enchantment with the world which for centuries has been presen-ted as the ultimate model of true civilization. Paralleling this disenchantment of the native American is the nonnative American's questioning of many of the basic premises of our own civilization. Of course this is evident on the part of significant segments of the society. It may thus be said that both Indian and non-Indian are now engaged in a quest for the roots of lost heritages now in-creasingly understood to be essential if we are to reorient our cultures and lives toward values which express real human nature. It may be that in the process of this mutual quest many of the native American groups are far closer to their sources than we are. And so perhaps for the first time in history we are allowing, even asking them to talk, so that we may listen and learn. Hope lies in the possibility of a true dialogue wherein each may learn from the other, so that each may come to know him or herself. We are essentially both engaged in the same kind of process, each in our own way asking the same kinds of fundamental questions. This is at least my hope.

The new search for the roots of traditions obscured or lost is today symptomatic in varying degrees for both native and nonnative Americans. Definitions of the causes for such respective self-examination and reevaluations are both simple and vastly complex. They are obvious yet elusive. This present statement then cannot pretend to be exhaustive, but is intended to be exploratory and suggestive. It proposes to identify certain root causes of the new awareness as these have become evident through an exploding array of literary productions by Indians and non-Indians and through news-media coverage of recent crises and frustrations. But this statement also issues from personal experiences of the writer over the past quarter of a century through close contacts with native peoples on and off the reservations, and with Indian and non-Indian students of schools and universities. It is hoped that if the root causes of the situation are grasped, or at least partially identified, it may be possible to place, and to relate with understanding to a multitude of those present events, movements, and phenomena which are unfolding with increasing intensity. New manifestations of Indian militancy, for example, may be responsible for increased public awareness. This is not an unimportant factor. But such action-oriented movements certainly neither define nor resolve the root causes of the problems. It would thus be superficial to assert as has often been suggested that action-oriented techniques are primarily responsible for the current renewal or reformulation of elements of a people's traditional heritage.

Account should also be taken, although analysis cannot be provided here, or the many native groups who have learned over many generations of bitter experiences to preserve their sacred traditions underground. Many elements of the current "renewal," therefore, represent the simple current willingness of the people to give greater visibility to their sacred rites and belief, which have been kept hidden from a materially dominant world intent on destroying these very traditions.

We are faced today, at least as it is viewed by the present writer, by what may be called a pervasive process on a global scale of detraditionalization or despiritualization. The world has been experiencing this process in a cumulative manner for many centuries. Exceedingly complex historical causes are no doubt responsible. This process of detraditionalization and its manifestations has had an impact on the integrity of virtually all native American traditions or lifeways. As this process of detraditionalization has proceeded its influence has demanded that the basic premises and orientations of our society be reevaluated. And in parallel manner we can perceive reevaluation of their own conditions by native peoples themselves. This includes an assessment of their relationships to the materially dominant society. When sincere attempt has been made by native people to adjust to or acculturate within the dominant society, they have become involved in a process of diminishing returns, or have reached dead-ends with regard to acquiring a meaningful quality of life.

We witness then the struggle of both Indian and non-Indian to find answers to their respective situations. Increasingly this search has led to attempts to regain contact with the roots of their respective traditions. Since their indigenous traditions are deeply and intricately rooted in this very land, unlike the situation of more recently transplanted Europeans, the Indian has a certain advantage in this contemporary quest. Furthermore, many of the ancient and sacred traditions of Indian groups are still living realities. They continue to provide viable systems of beliefs, values, and lifeways to give meaning, dignity, and wholeness to life. In the current growing awareness of this situation it is understandable that non-native peoples, especially among the younger generations who once looking everywhere for answers except to their own homeland are now increasingly turning to native peoples and their traditions for possible alternatives to the values of their own society. To them such values have come to represent a world of impoverished reality. The great hope in this dual search on the part of Indian and non-Indian is that a true and open dialogue may be established through which neither will attempt to imitate the other, but where each may ultimately regain and reaffirm the sacred dimensions of *their own* respective traditions.

In spite of the vast differences between native cultures of North America with their respective sacred traditions, it is nevertheless deemed possible for the purpose of this statement to identify certain core or root themes which seem to undergird the traditions of all these groups even though they are expressed through a rich diversity of means. More precisely it may be said that across this diversity and at a certain level, we are in fact dealing with what may be called dialects of a common language of the sacred. In speaking in that which follows of such core themes underlying native traditions, themes which have come to speak with special force to the general conditions of today, the distinctions between these themes and their contrasting counterparts in the contemporary non-Indian world should be self-evident and need not in all cases be directly pointed to. What then are these native themes which may speak to the deep unrest and concerns of these times?

Time

Within traditional native American cultures, time tends to be experienced as cyclical and rhythmic rather than as lineal and "progress"-oriented. The rhythm of the world in its mode of operation is believed to be circular, as the life of man or the life of any manifested form, being, or a cyclical period within larger cycles. Events or processes transmitted through oral traditions tend to be recounted neither in terms of time past or time future in a lineal sense. Indeed most native languages have no such tenses to express this. They speak rather to a perennial reality of the now. The rich mythic accounts of creation, for example, are not so much of chronological time-past as they usually tend to be read by us. Rather they tell of processes which are of eternal happening; the same processes are recurring now and are to recur in other cycles.

Given this structure of experience, supported by the forms of language, and made immediate through experienced interrelationships with the elements of each people's natural environment, it is impossible to conceive of progress in the contemporary non-Indian lineal sense in native American thought. We refer to the quantitatively interpreted cumulative process in which the more and the "new" mysteriously and automatically become identified with the better. The actual forces and events asserting themselves upon us at this present moment in our history, however, increasingly demand a backward look at progress so that such promises may be reexamined critically. Through such reexamination and possible reorientation, it may become possible for native American traditions to serve as a reminder of forgotten or neglected dimensions latent within the European American's own heritage. We know that at one time this heritage also manifested a dependence on sacred time.

Place

If alternatives are being sought today to our pervasive lineal, progress-laden concepts of time, there is also the parallel quest for a new understanding and appreciation of place. Speaking to this search, again, are those native American affirmations of the interrelated sacredness of time and place. This is spelled out across our land with enormous creative diversity. Yet all of it exhibits some fundamental common principles. There is a strong message here. It relates to the new willingness on the part of certain non-Indians to listen to those whose roots are deep and long within this land.

Native experiences of place are infused with mythic themes. These express events of sacred time, which are as real now as in any time. They are experienced through each landmark of each people's immediate natural environment. The events of animal beings, for example, which are communicated through oral traditions of myths or "folklore," serve to grace, sanctify, explain, and interpret each detail of the land. Further, each being of nature, every particular form of the land, is experienced as the locus of qualitatively differentiated spirit-beings, whose individual and collective presence sanctifies and gives meaning to the land in all its details and contours. Thus, it also gives meaning to the life of man who cannot conceive of himself apart from the land. Such beliefs in a plurality of indwelling spirits (often referred to rather unkindly as "animism" or "animatism"), must be understood in relation to a polysynthetic quality of vision. The recognition of multiplicity on one level of reality need not militate against the coalescing of the omnipresent spirit-beings within a more ultimate unitary principle. Such a polysynthetic metaphysic of nature, immediately experienced rather than dangerously abstracted, speaks with particular force to the root causes of many of today's problems, especially to our present so-called "ecological crisis." It is perhaps this message of the sacred nature of the land, of place, that today has been most responsible for forcing the native American vision upon the mind and conscience of the non-Indian.

Such affirmation and experience of sacred time and sacred place wherever this may be found tends to free humanity from the oppressive limits, the prison, of profane time, and profane place. Experiencing such constriction and thus inevitably feeling nostalgia for what has been lost, people today have come to seek the illusion of liberation through explorations of "outer space." This quest is futile of course, especially if embarked upon to satisfy ultimate concerns, since even such seemingly limitless reaches of space, being always of a material and thus quantitative order, are still within the domain of limitation. Such attempts by contemporary men to "conquer" time and space, even to "conquer" specific places, are incomprehensible to native Americans, particularly to native American or arctic shamans. These shamans through the nonmaterial means of their sacred traditions are able to travel at will through the freedom of sacred space unfettered by mechanical, profane time.

Not only native Americans but traditionally oriented peoples wherever they may be always found the means by which to be protected from the indefinity of space. The tipi, the hogan, or the long house, just as the temple, cathedral, or those sacred city centers of antiquity determined the perimeters of space in such a way that a sacred place, or enclosure, was established. Space so defined served as a model of the world, of the universe, or microcosmically, of a human being. Essential to such definition of space, so central to human need, were means by which the centers of sacred space of place were established. For without such ritual fixing of a center there can be no circumference. And with neither circumference nor center where does a person stand? A ritually defined center, whether the fire at the center of the plains tipi or the *sipapu* (earth navel) within the Pueblo *kiva*, obviously expresses not just a mathematically fixed point established arbitrarily in space. It is also taken to be the actual center of the world. It is understood as an axis serving as a bridge between heaven and earth, an axis that pierces through a multiplicity of worlds. The great cottonwood tree at the center of (and branching out above) the Plains Sun Dance lodge is this central axis. It symbolizes the way of liberation from the limits of the cosmos. Always, vertical ascent is impossible unless the starting point be the ritual center. The problem is to recover the meanings of such forms and ritual acts by whatever tradition they may be represented. Here again such primordial types of formulations found within our American land may serve as reminders to those who have lost or forgotten the sense of a center.

Relationship

One key to the native religious perspective, which again speaks to a quality of life sought by contemporary generations in their loss of center and concomitant sense of alienation and fragmentation, may be found in native American concepts of the experience of relationship. The structuring of such native relationships of all orders are richly defined and supported by the forms of language and by specific ritual means. Relationships between members of family, band, clan, or tribal groups tend to be defined, thus intensified, through relational or generational terms rather than through personal names which were considered to be sacred and thus private to the individual. This sense of relationship pertained not only to members of a nuclear family, band, or clan. It also extended ever outwards to include all beings of the specific environment, the elements and the winds, whether these beings, forms, or powers are what we would call animate or inanimate. In native thought no such hard dichotomies exist. All such forms under creation were understood to be mysteriously interrelated. Everything was as a relative to every other being or "thing." Thus, nothing existed in isolation. The intricately interrelated threads of the spider's web was referred to depict the world. The same reference occurs in native American art. This is a profound "symbol," when it is understood. The people obviously observed that the threads of the web were drawn out from within the spider's very being. They also recognized that the threads in concentric circles were sticky whereas the threads leading to the center were smooth!

One vivid example of this comprehensive sense of relationship is expressed with special force among the Plains peoples in rites involving communal smoking of the pipe. At the conclusion of the pipe ceremony among the Lakota the participants all exclaim: "We are all related!" Acknowledged here is not only the relatedness of the immediate participating group. There is also an affirmation of the mysterious interrelatedness of all that is. The rites of the pipe make specific mention of the fact that each of the indefinite number of grains of tobacco placed in the bowl of the pipe represents ritually, or really *is*, some specific form or possibility of creation. The act of smoking then is a rite of communion. Through the agency of man's breath the apparent multiplicity and separateness of phenomena (the tobacco) is absorbed within an ultimate unity (the fire).

If new life is being given to these kinds of rites among native peoples today, or to any similar means for the reaffirmation of relationship, belonging, and identity, it is entirely understandable. Many of the people to whom this has happened have either been denied truly meaningful relationships with the dominant society, or have found frustration in a society where experience is so excessively and artificially fragmented. Here again native traditions are speaking with special force both to contemporary problems of the peoples themselves, as well as to the concerns of the larger society in its fragmentation, to the individual's sense of alienation, and, above all, to the recognition of the loss of Center.

The Oral Traditions

Perhaps the greatest tragedy to come upon native American groups has been the progressive weakening and occasional total loss of their respective languages. Since it is language which supports and communicates the total range of a people's values and worldview, it was realized early by the dominant society that native languages must be supplanted by the language of the dominant society if cultural assimilation was to occur. The history of the frequent brutal means by which this process of deculturation was furthered need not be reiterated here. We must stress the fact, however, that due to the inherent persistence of language many native languages have survived. Furthermore, many native American groups are taking deliberate measures to insure that these languages are both recovered and used.

These procedures are being assisted by the increasing control native Americans are exercising with respect to their own educational systems. Where such languages are alive, possibilities exist that oral traditions can be revitalized to communicate the core values to all members of the group. Concomitant with the Indian's reassessment of the meaning and values of such oral traditions is a certain new appreciation for and understanding of the value of such traditions by some segments of the dominant society. This society has always placed a very high premium on literacy and on the lineal perspective, which in this case means the written line. In this new evaluation recognition is finally being given to the powerful effectiveness of oral transmission for educational purposes. Certain elements of the effectiveness may be seen in the importance given to the "frame," that is, the time, the season, and the immediate environment within which the narration takes place. All of this serves to place, reinforce, and intensify that which is communicated. Regardless of the type of myth or "folktale," multiple levels of understanding are always possible. This enables the narration to speak specifically and simultaneously to all age groups present. Normally in tribal societies the elders of experience serve as repositories for the oral lore of the people. Living oral traditions give the elders of the society a position of respect and importance among their people. Further, since oral tradition also speaks even to the youngest in the group, it creates bridges of understanding between the generations. Oral tradition can thus be addressed with special force to problems of generational segmentation and individual alienation so typical of much of the American world today.

It is a trait of the Southwestern Pueblo peoples to objectify the realities and dynamics of experience through the *kachinas*, sometimes called "gods". There is an account of a Zuni kachina who emerged from the underworld attached back to back with a person from an alien world. Back to back, it was suggested, the alien is destined neither to see nor understand the Zuni. Yet the fact remains that the two are attached. If there is hope, it lies in the possibility that there may come a time for a turning around, so that each may know who the other is and what the other might become.

3

Hopi Indian Ceremonies

EMORY SEKAQUAPTEWA

I do not intend here to make any claims about religion in a scholarly sense. I simply want to talk about a personal experience and what significance it has in my present world. As with most of us, I have become aware of the new interest in cultural pluralism. I find that in this new atmosphere of awareness many people, especially American Indians, are attempting to strengthen their identity within their cultural background. But this is responsible for some unfortunate results. There are many who have lost touch with their culture, and they are trying now to recapture what they have lost, unable to resort to something they already are and to strengthen it from within. I am concerned personally about how I have made my adjustment to the dominant society (which is the term we use). It is in this area that I have attempted to set down guidelines which might be of some help to those who find adjustment and adaptation difficult. I am going to try to illustrate my point of view by giving an impression and interpretation of some Hopi ceremonies. I have chosen this to illustrate how it happens that attitudes are developed in the child. In particular, I want to talk about the *kachina* ceremony, with which I am most familiar. My remarks are of an autobiographical nature.

I was born and raised in a small Hopi village. My first language, of course, was Hopi. In the world I first came to know, I had various experiences which resulted in images by which I knew the world around me. One of these very significant and prominent images, as I recall my early childhood, is the kachina doll. It developed particular meaning for me.

In Hopi practice the kachina is represented as a real being. From the time children are able to understand and to verbalize, until they are eight or ten years old, they are taught that the kachina is real. Every exposure the child has to the kachina is to a spiritual being which is real. There are a variety of ways in which the Hopis attempt to demonstrate this realism to the child. The kachina is all goodness and all kindness. The kachina also gives gifts to children in all of its appearances. Thus it is rather difficult for me to agree with the descriptions of the kachina that often appear in literature. The kachina is frequently described as being grotesque, but the Hopi child does not perceive the kachina as grotesque.

By his conduct toward the child, the kachina demands good behavior. As children we were taught that all things that come from the Kachina hold certain spiritual gifts of reproduction. That is to say, when we received a bowl of fruit or something else, the gift was brought home and placed in the middle of the room. We were then given cornmeal and asked to go outside the house and pray in our childish fashion for an abundance of what we had received. And when we came back into the house, there was more than we had actually received from the hand of the kachina. This kind of practice builds in Hopi children the notion of the kachina as the symbol of ideal goodness.

Then there are times when the kachina is the symbol of admonition. When the child misbehaves he or she is threatened either with the idea that the kachinas will withhold their kindness from them, or even that the kachinas will come and deprive them of their person. There are various ways to dramatize this. I recall a little skit, which was performed to appease the kachina *soya*. The soya has been described as an ogre, but this is a misnomer. The soya is used to threaten the child because of bad behavior, but it certainly does not appear as an ogre to the child. So I prefer to say soya, which is the name of this kachina. He appears at a certain time of the year; and in preparation for his appearance certain children are given a warning. If they do not behave, straighten up, the kachina will come and take them. But threats as such are never effective unless there is some mechanism by which the child can appreciate and understand how one can get out of this predicament. So, in preparation for the appearance of the soya to the child, the parents plan or design a scheme by which they are going to save the child at the very last moment. The one which was used in the case I am talking about was this: the child, barely six years old, had misbehaved and was threatened with the appearance of the soya, who would come and take him away because he had misbehaved. So on the day of the arrival of the kachina, the parents had planned that when the kachinas came to the door, they would send the child outside, and the mother would appear with the child and inform the kachina in all seriousness that it was not right and timely for them to come after him, because he was going to be married. He was a groom and until this very important ceremony was completed he was not available. So the kachinas demanded some proof. They were very persistent, so after much drama and emotion the bride was brought out to show that there really was a marriage ceremony going on. The bride turned out to be the old grandmother, who was dressèd in the full paraphernalia of a bride. Then bride and groom appealed as a pair to the kachinas that this was indeed an important ceremony. Obviously when there is a marriage, the relations on both sides are very interested in the preservation of the union. So all the relatives intervened, and soon they outnumbered the kachinas, and thus the child was saved. The child not only learned the importance of good behavior, but this drama also strengthened his security by showing him that there are people who do come to his aid.

This is just an attempt to point out the various ways the child is brought up to feel and know security. Security comes from knowing one's place within the prevailing kinship relationship; within the community. But it also involves learning the cultural norms or the community ethic.

Then comes a time when the child has demonstrated a certain degree of responsibility and understanding, when he or she shows the ability to comprehend a little more of the spiritual world. At this time they are ready to be initiated into the kachina ceremony. This ceremony is quite elaborate and is intended to expose the young person* to what the kachina is in fact and in spirit, attempting to help him discern the difference between the spirit and the fact. He learns that he has become eligible to participate in the kachina dance like his father, his brothers, his uncles, whom he has held in high regard. Now he is going to participate as one of them. He learns to identify with the adult world in this fashion. Because this is done in such a dramatic way he has a good foundation. When it is revealed to him that the kachina is just an impersonation, an impersonation which possesses a spiritual essence, the child's security is not destroyed. Instead the experience strengthens the individual in another phase of his life in the community.

Since the kachina has been so prominent in the child's life, most of the child's fantasies involve the kachina. Before his initiation most of his fantasies have consisted in emulating the kachina. Children go around the corner of the house; they enact their feelings about the kachina, they dance and sing like the kachina. At this early age they begin to feel the sense of projection into this spiritual reality. When the child is initiated and becomes eligible to participate as a kachina, it is not difficult to fantasize now as a participant in the real kachina ceremony, and that is the essence of the kachina ceremony. The fantasizing continues, then, in spite of the initiation which seems to have the effect of revealing to the child that this is just a plaything, that now we are grown up and we don't believe.

* While I describe this initiation from my own experience as a young boy, both girls and boys participate in this ceremony.

This idea of make-believe continues with the Hopi man and woman as they mature, and as far as I am concerned it must continue throughout life. For the kachina ceremonies require that a person project oneself into the spirit world, into the world of fantasy, or the world of make-believe. Unless one can do this, spiritual experience cannot be achieved.

I am certain that the use of the mask in the kachina ceremony has more than just an esthetic purpose. I feel that what happens to a man when he is performer is that if he understands the essence of the kachina, when he dons the mask he loses his identity and actually becomes what he is representing. Of course there are various circumstances created to help him to make this projection: the circumstances connected with the ceremony itself, in addition to the individual's background of exposure to the kachina ceremony from childhood. The spiritual fulfillment of a man depends on how he he is able to project himself into the spiritual world as he performs. He really doesn't perform for the third parties who form the audience. Rather the audience becomes his personal self. He tries to express to himself his own conceptions about the spiritual ideals that he sees in the kachina. He is able to do so behind the mask because he has lost his personal identity. He is less inhibited by the secular world and its institutions, all of which inhibit people. I think this is a very important element in the kachina ceremonies. The idea of performing to yourself is a rather difficult one for me to describe in terms of a theory. I would have difficulty were I asked to give concrete answers to questions about religious belief and experience. But the essence of the kachina ceremony for me as a participant has to do with the ability to project oneself into the make-believe world, the world of ideas and images which sustain that particular representation.

Now what does all this mean with reference to the issues we talked about earlier? What does it say about cultural backgrounds? How does it apply to identity questions? How can it prepare one for the modern world of technology and all the consequences of life in an affluent society? This is a particular area of concern to me.

I have attempted to understand, first, for myself, what one can do when he knows himself to be an Indian in an Indian culture and then goes into an affluent society which operates according to very different values. Anthropologists have attempted to identify and understand the various means of assimilation and acculturation, such as incorporation, assimilation, diffusion, and lately, compartmentalization. But the problem remains a difficult one.

I don't know how to offer clarification in scientific terms. But I do feel that a process of compartmentalization is necessary for an Indian coming out of his own cultural environment into another cultural situation. Compartmentalization—or keeping the two worlds separate and distinct—is necessary if the American Indian is to make the proper adjustments and adaptations. I think that many people who come from one cultural situation to another share this problem. The problem stems from the compulsion they feel to make the proper adjustments by becoming like the members of the dominant society. The notion of compartmentalization argues that one need not reject his cultural values to make an adjustment to an alien situation. Instead one tries to put his own cultural values in abeyance while he participates in the other culture, perhaps participating only in form and not in substance. But nevertheless his conduct and behavior fit the alien situation so that he himself becomes inconspicuous, while his values remain elsewhere. This is perhaps the layman's explanation of the theory of compartmentalization.

It is to this situation that I have attempted to address myself. I have done this because I know that, as Indian people, we have come to realize the importance of rediscovering ourselves or strengthening ourselves. And I have watched with great interest the way in which Indians across the country have manifested their own interest in their Indianness. This interest has manifested itself in a wide range of attitudes from the sort of disinterested, passive attitude to highly motivated militant aggressiveness. And there are a variety of possibilities inbetween. I have attempted to look at this situation and see why there is such a wide range of attitudes. I am sure that the goal is the same: it is to retain and preserve and strengthen the Indian culture. It is my belief that those Indians who have retained their own cultural values to the highest degree are not concerned with convincing anyone that they are Indians. Those who, for various reasons have not been able to retain their cultural values are quite concerned with convincing their audience that they are Indians. It is manifested through an aggressive attitude and an intense effort to prove to the world that "I am Indian."

As a result, we have come recently to see a development of pan-Indianism. This is something new to an Indian whose only experience is within his own tribal culture. "Indian" is certainly a term which was confusing from the beginning. To the non-Indian, "Indian" may have some validity. But it does not derive from a particular Indian culture. It is something which has been concocted by the non-Indian. He has put together various characteristics of Indians across the country and has produced a new image, which is a stereotype Indian. It is a stereotype, and not an accurate reflection of our empirical reality. It is something which has been created or constructed as a representation of the Indian. In terms of bringing awareness of the Indian to the non-Indian, it serves well. Once the non-Indian becomes aware of the existence of Indians and the richness of their cultures, then he is ready to become interested in a specific tribe of Indians. If this is what is happening, then it is a good thing.

I have often wondered, however, whether we should be convincing the white man that we are Indians. I feel that we should be convincing ourselves and strengthening ourselves in our own cultural values. I really get a little frustrated when I see Indians attempting to straighten out facts about Indians. They are attempting to destroy the stereotype, because they want the non-Indian to know the truth about the Indian. They are more concerned about that than about strengthening the cultural values that come from within the Indian culture. I think that the latter is the more important for us to be concerned about. We are certainly intimidated by the attitude that is taken by the non-Indian. The Indian has become a national symbol of certain things. For example, he has become a hero lately in our corporate concern for ecological balance. In our concern about environmental pollution, the Indian has become a symbol of conservation. This I think, is good. However, if one were to ask an Indian (to whom is attributed a special knowledge about conservation and harmony with nature) some pointed questions on this subject, he cannot expect that the Indian will be able to explain harmony to you in analytical and scientific terms.

I recall a problem of this sort in a school operated under the Bureau of Indian affairs. These days there are various programs either coming through the Bureau of Indian affairs or funded through the bureau and contracted with other agencies, state and federal. These projects are presumably intended to help the child to understand and become better adjusted to the school system of the white man, thus to be in position to experience a little more success. One of these programs was a science project, a study of ecology. The teachers at the school implemented the project by means of the guidelines given them. It called for the children to bring various living things (insects, animals, etc.) into the classroom, putting them in a cage and accepting responsibility for their care while they watched what happened. It seems that the Hopi children were not interested in taking care of the animals while they studied them. It didn't matter to them whether the animals died or survived. The teachers became very concerned about how to teach the Hopi child about ecology if he didn't show any interest. He had no feeling for the animal.

We never resolved the problem as far as the teachers are concerned. But I would like to make the statement that perhaps ecology, or learning how to live with the environment, is not a matter of taking sides with one or some other living things; rather it is acceptance of the fact that if a certain living thing cannot survive on its own, that is a fact. Must we intervene with our special powers as human beings to control and bring about ways to help this poor thing to survive outside its natural ability to survive? And I talk about pets—cats and dogs—who are treated like human beings in the Anglo household and society. They are really deprived of their natural instincts; they become very dependent on the human beings. Indians don't keep their dogs in the house. The dog which becomes a pet of an Indian family really has a great responsibility to survive on his own, as well as on occasion to depend on his master for things. What I am trying to say is that learning to live with the environment is not a matter of taking sides, but of accepting facts. It seems to me that this attitude and the conduct of the Indian is the only way that he is able to communicate with the people who are concerned about conservation, but not always in verbal ways. We sometimes get overly scholarly about these things, and we tend to build up reputations about Indians in our own terms, rather than stopping and just listening for awhile, watching and seeing what happens, to see if we can make any sense of that kind of communication coming from the Indian.

4

The Shadow of a Vision Yonder

SAM D. GILL

Several summers ago while my family and I were living with a Navajo family north of Tuba City, Arizona, I witnessed an ordinary social event that at the time I thought to be curious but of little consequence. Since then I have found occasion to reflect upon that event. From it I think I learned something about the Navajo way of life, even something about their religion, which is the subject I had gone there to pursue. I confess that I went to the Navajo reservation not very well prepared to do fieldwork. I had not done enough homework to afford me the clearest view of my contact with Navajo people. As a result, much of what I was to learn came to me through insightful flashbacks sometime after I had left Navajo country.

By midsummer we had become well enough acquainted with our Navajo family to be trusted with some of their work. I considered it an honor to be asked to help hoe the weeds in the cornfield they had planted in the valley below the beautiful mesa on which we lived. Being from a farming family in Kansas, I willingly accepted the invitation and replied that I would gladly hoe the corn.

To my dismay our Navajo friends expressed alarm. I am sure they were considering how they could retract the invitation as they told me, "Oh no, we don't hoe the *corn*, we hoe the weeds!" I assured them that I really did know the difference between corn plants and the unwanted weeds and that it was just the way we described the job back home. It was simply a product of the peculiarity of my own language, not theirs.

After getting the younger children on their way with the sheep, we headed for the cornfield early the next morning. Under cautious eyes, I set about proving that I not only knew the difference between weeds and corn, but that I was no slouch with a hoe. Of course, I was never to know the extent of my success. The weight of my experience with the Navajo people is that their quiet dignity always prevails.

With my flashing hoe gradually slowing to match the ordered, rhythmic movement of the other hoes—the native hoes—I was relieved when late in the morning it was time to stop for lunch. Moving to the arbor or "shade", a small partly enclosed brush structure, we took lunch. Then we prepared to rest for several hours during the heat of the day. It was in the shade that I was to observe the event on which I want to reflect.

The shade was perhaps half a mile from a narrow dirt road. In that part of the country the traffic is not what one would call heavy. During the quiet rest period after lunch, I was aroused from my drowsiness a couple of times by a soft but excited discussion of whatever motor vehicle, usually a pickup truck, passed by on the road. I noticed that all present expressed interest in the traffic. They arose and peered through the open areas in the brush on the side of the shade facing the road. I recalled the many times I had driven up to a Navajo dwelling, finding absolutely no sign of human activity.

What surprised me was the response my friends made when one of the passing pickups turned off the road and headed toward our shade. Watching with rapt attention, my Navajo friends carefully timed it so that as the truck pulled up to the shade and stopped, every member of the family was actively occupied. The grandmother sat on the ground with her back to the entrance near the truck and began her spinning. The children played a game in the dirt of the shade floor. Others sat about, gazing across the landscape, always in a direction away from the truck. This directed all attention away from the presence of the visitors.

The visitors in the truck were Navajos and knew how to respond. They sat in the truck for some minutes. It seemed like a very long time to me. Then quietly, the man, his wife and young daughter left their truck to enter the edge of the shade. There they sat upon the ground. The man quietly restrained the eagerness of the little girl to play with the other children. Again some minutes passed while my family continued their spinning, playing, and gazing. Finally, the man spoke a few soft words to the grandmother, who gently, almost inaudibly, responded without turning her head toward him. In a few moments he spoke again. This quiet conversation continued for some time, then the visitors arose and moved about the shade, talking softly to each of us, including me, extending their hands for a handshake and speaking the Navajo greeting, "yá'át'ééh." Next my friends arose and began to intermingle with the visitors. I was informed that they were going to the trading post some ten miles away to get water and supplies to prepare a meal for the visitors. The entire proceedings had taken more than a quarter of an hour.

The insight that has come to me through continued reflection is that the incident illustrates the "way" of Navajo religion. I had witnessed the performance of a formal ritual for purposes of establishing certain kinds of social relationships, in this instance, between Navajo families. The ritual reflects the quiet dignity and the patient and formal manner of the Navajo people. And by its simplicity it helps place the almost infinite complexity of Navajo ceremonies in a better perspective. It also gives clues regarding the nature of Navajo religion, wherein relationships are established or reestablished with the holy ones.

Notice that the situation had been carefully analyzed by my

Navajo friends. They followed proper conduct with deliberateness and patience. This resulted in the successful establishing of a relationship between two families. Each party made some sign to show that it understood its obligations and was committing itself to their fulfillment. The guests offered their hands as a sign of their entrance into the relationship. My family proceeded to meet their first obligation of the relationship by offering a meal to the guests.

It is commonly observed that Navajo religion centers largely upon the rituals by which an individual who is suffering a malady is healed. The sufferer is attended to by an individual called a "singer". The "singer" directs the ritual activities and is responsible for knowing the songs, prayers, and the order of the ritual processes. A Navajo ceremony is not performed unless it is called for. But when it is called for, the family of the sufferer must arrange with a "singer" to perform the ceremony. This requires making a formal relationship through social and ritual acts not unlike those characteristic of the introduction to which I have made reference. In both settings the relationship is bonded through a formal sign. In this case the "singer" receives payment in material goods or in cash in return for performing the ceremony. David Aberle has analyzed this exchange and has convincingly shown that the "fee" is not really payment for services rendered, but is a sign of the establishment of a reciprocity relationship.[1] The "singer" is thus obliged to respond by conducting the requested ceremonial.

In the performance of Navajo ceremonies, the observer is struck by the material insignificance of the ritual objects. He also cannot help but notice the extreme care and formality with which these objects are treated. A singer's medicine bundle consists of nothing more precious than an odd assortment of sticks, feathers, bags of colored sands and vegetal materials, rocks, and so on. These things appear so common, even crude, that it makes one wonder how they could have any religious significance. But in the context of ritual the same objects are carefully handled, described in song, explicated in prayer, and manipulated in ritual. Their significance is developed to such a magnitude that they infinitely surpass their material content in signifying that which the Navajo regards as being holy.

This is in keeping with the story of creation in Navajo mythology. The story utilizes common objects in describing the process of bringing life to the world. First Man, who directed the creation, had a medicine bundle containing bits of colored rocks, called "jewels." First Man carefully placed these "jewels" upon the floor of the creation hogan to designate the life forces of the things which were to be created. All life forms were represented in these mundane substances, and their distinguishing characteristics were understood to be exemplified in the shapes of the jewels. Furthermore, the relative place where each was laid on the floor of the creation hogan designated the place each was to occupy in the world, together with the relationship each was to have to all other living things. These material representations of life were then clothed in a layer of colored sands to represent the outward appearance they would have in the created world. After the preparation of this symbolic mircocosm has been completed, prayers were uttered to transform the symbolic creation into the more visible everyday world of the Navajos. This is the way in which the Navajos conceive the process of the creation of their world. When creation was completed the world was beautiful. All things were formed and set in a place, and proper relationships existed between them.

In both the creation of the world and in the creation of the social relationships formalities dominate. The formal enactment of ritual brings things to their proper place and serves to interconnect them by establishing binding relationships. Ritual acts are understood to be essential to the establishing of proper relationships. Navajo life depends upon such relationships.

Scholarly interpretation doesn't always catch the significance of this. Frequently, the interpretation of Navajo religion has called attention to the performance of "magical" acts. They are called "magical" to indicate that there is no ordinary causal principle which connects the acts performed with the expected results. I would never want to dismiss the presence of mystery and magic in Navajo religion. Yet it seems to me that the more significant factor is the process by which the visions and great conceptions are communicated by the formal manipulation of mundane objects. Let me illustrate the difference. The most common scholarly interpretation of the sandpainting rite is that it contains a kind of magical osmosis. The sandpainting is prepared upon the floor of the ceremonial hogan, the patient enters and sits upon the sandpainting, and the singer applies sands from the figures represented in the sandpainting to the patient. At the conclusion of the rite, the sandpaintings are formally destroyed and removed from the ceremonial hogan. According to the "magical osmosis" explanation, the sandpainting is understood to absorb the illness, or the evil cause of the illness, taking it from the patient and replacing it with goodness from the sandpainting. This explanation focuses attention on the removal of the sands after the rite, for it resembles and builds upon similarities between this act and the removal of sands into which one vomits in emetic rites.

In my view, this "magical osmosis" interpretation is partial. I would propose instead that sandpainting rites are meaningful curing acts because of the Navajos' recognition of the *performative* powers of symbolic representation. In preparing the sandpainting, the Navajos follow the precedent established in the processes of world creation. In Navajo mythology it is said that "in the beginning" the forces of life were set forth in material form by arranging common objects of several colors upon the floor of a ceremonial hogan. Thus, in physical representations using ordinary materials, Navajos express their conception of the profound nature of life. In a healing ceremony the sandpaintings are closely associated with the elements identified with the cause of the illness suffered. As is told in the mythology of each ceremonial, the sandpaintings are revealed to the mythic hero as he is being cured of an illness. In most cases the illness is due to the fact that something is out of its proper place. For example, a ghost who will not remain in its domain, a person who has made contact with the dead, a deity who has been angered or offended by a person who has trespassed or violated a taboo, or a witch who has gained power by being out of bounds. The causal agent rather than the illness suffered determines the nature of the ceremonial cure. The ritual presents the forces of life in the shape and relative places assigned to them by sacred history as recounted in the myths. The identification of the patient with the sandpainting by touching the sands of the parts of the body of the painted figures to the corresponding parts of the patient is a gesture of communicating *proper relationships* to the patient. This is very similar to the acts performed to place the forces of life represented on the floor of the creation hogan within the representations of the outward forms they were to take in the real world. And, as in the case of the process of world creation, the formal removal of the sandpaintings designates a transition from the world of ritual to the world thus represented. This transition illustrates that reality is dynamic and will not always be contained in symbolic form.

Relationships are central to the Navajo way of life. Life's interrelationships are not casual. They are the product of careful ritual prescription, which acts both to bind and reestablish a proper order of relationships. In the Navajo conception, life and good health are not so much a matter of substance—for all things belong to the earth—as they are a matter of form and place with respect to the rest of the created world. Each living thing has an identity, a proper place, and a way to be. This identity, place, and way must be honored and carefully maintained.

The Navajo way of life can be characterized at one level as a kind of symbolic formalism, although Navajos would not describe it in these terms. The Navajos' own appreciation of symbolization becomes particularly compelling in their belief about the curative power of the healing rites. Here the symbols presented are appreciated for having the power to cure physical illness; and the Navajo have in mind something quite different from our common reduction of their religion to a kind of primitive psychology. In the symbols of their religion they recognize a power to change the shape of things in the world, even when the materials which compose the symbols are mundane. This performative power stems from a religious tradition that takes form in ritual acts. Such acts make earthly elements into a vehicle disclosing the deepest forces of life.

Navajo symbols within sandpainting rites are comparable to the shaking of hands to seal a social relationship. Both of these acts reflect the same temperament. Both indicate the way in which Navajos apprehend reality. In both cases, mundane ingredients find deeper symbolic significance. There is nothing special in the handshake, for example. But in the context of the formal ritual of establishing relationships, handshaking performs an essential role by assuring each party of the acceptance of the privileges and obligations of the relationship. It marks transformation from a relationship discussed to a relationship established and made operative. Similarly, in Navajo sandpainting rites the substance of the colored sands is not as important as the shapes which they form. Properly prepared and used, the sandpainting has the power to cure. It reestablishes the patient with the forces of life on which his health and happiness depend. In this regard, one of the most important components of native American religions is the process by which concepts of being and becoming are represented and communicated through the use of symbols. I have cited one instance of this in Navajo religion. We can find the same phenomenon when we turn to Hopi culture.

I remember feeling confused when I learned that Hopi children witness an event which they find shocking and bitterly disappointing at the conclusion of their first religious initiation. I am referring to the conclusion of the initiation into the kachina cult which is composed of two societies, the Kachina Society and the Powamu Society. Formally, this initiation begins the religious life of all Hopi children, boys and girls alike. The event occurs as a part of the Bean Dance which concludes the annual celebration of Powamu, a late winter ceremonial to prepare for the agricultural cycle. The newly initiated children are escorted into a kiva, an underground ceremonial chamber, there to await the entrance of the kachinas, the masked dancers they have come to know as Hopi gods. Prior to this time, the already initiated go to great efforts to keep the children from discovering that kachinas are masked male members of their own village. Announcing that they are kachinas, the dancers enter the kiva where the children are eagerly awaiting them. But they appear for the first time to the new initiates without their masks. The children immediately recognize the identity of the dancing figures. Their response is shock, disappointment, and bitterness. Don Talayesva, an old Oraibi Hopi, recalled his feelings at the time of his initiation in his autobiography *Sun Chief*.

> When the Katcinas entered the kiva without masks, I had a great surprise. They were not spirits, but human beings. . . . I had been told all my life that the Katcinas were gods. I was especially shocked and angry when I saw all my uncles, fathers, and clan brothers dancing as Katcinas (84).

It would seem to me that this concluding event in the Powamu ceremonial leaves the children in a peculiarly unstable state as new initiates. I would have expected the purpose of the initiation to reveal clearly the full nature of the kachinas to the children. But it appears that the initiation rites accomplish only the destruction of the belief in the identity of the kachina figures as gods, as it was held by the children prior to initiation. I understand that Margaret Mead likened this event to the European-American child learning of the identity of Santa Claus, which is often accompanied by the same kind of bitter disappointment. There are surface similarities, but this is not a satisfactory explanation. Nor should we accept another scholarly interpretation that it is inevitable the children learn that kachinas are "not real gods, but men dressed as gods." We may find some force in this argument, since, as outside occasional observers, we can easily recognize that the kachina dancers are masked mortals. Even when we hear a Hopi say that when in donning the kachina mask he "becomes the kachina," we tend to offer a critical interpretation. Another older position dismisses the statement as primitive nonsense, regarding it as a product of a primitive mentality not skilled in precise distinctions. Then too, a play theory has been advanced. This position argues that the Hopi acts "as if" he were a kachina and makes the statement while he is so pretending. But all of these interpretations are found wanting.

Instead, it is important that we take seriously what the initiated Hopi says. We must recognize that he actually means what he says, that in putting on the kachina mask he really becomes a god. This is a clear statement on his part. It is in light of this statement that we should attempt to see how at the conclusion of the initiation the shadow cast upon the kachina figures serves to reveal to the children the true nature of the kachinas. The ceremony appears to be deliberately calculated to engender the disappointment the children feel.

A fuller review of the contextual events is necessary. Prior to the initiation into the kachina cult, the children largely under the age of ten are carefully guided into the development of a particular kind of relationship with the kachinas. The kachinas, who frequent the villages during only half of the year, have a wide range of contacts with the children. Many of them are kind and benevolent to the children, presenting them with gifts. Others are frightening ogres who discipline naughty children by threatening to eat them. And some are silly clowns who entertain the children with their antics. In all these contacts the uninitiated children are protected against seeing kachinas unmasked or the masks unoccupied. They are also guarded against hearing anything which might disclose the masked character of the kachina figures. The children are told that the kachinas are gods who come to the village from their homes far away to overlook and direct the affairs of the Hopi people. They are taught that they too will become kachinas when they die. Prior to the initiation events, the children grow to accept the familiar kachina figures as being exactly what they appear to be.

The perspective nurtured in the children is given its final stage of development in the kachina cult initiation rites. During the Powamu ceremonial to which the initiation rites are attached, the initiates are given special attention by the kachinas. They come into closer contact. The kachina give the children special gifts. They are instructed in kachina lore. All of this seems to be carefully calculated to intensify the shock the children will feel when they observe the unmasked appearance of the kachinas during the Bean Dance.

When the kachinas enter the kiva, in one sharp and sudden blow the expectations so carefully nurtured are forever shattered. For the moment only pain and bitterness take its place, as is evident in the statement of a Hopi woman quoted by Dorothy Eggan in her 1943 study of Hopi adjustment.

> I cried and cried into my sheepskin, that night, feeling I had been made a fool of. How could I ever watch the Kachinas dance again? I hated my parents and thought I would never believe the old folks said, wondering if Gods had ever danced for the Hopi as they said and if people really lived afetr death (372).

But even with the disappointment life goes on, and the initiated is given the privilege to participate in religious events. In time, the initiated can enter other religious societies and enjoy expanded privileges of participation. But once initiated into the kachina cult, religious events can never again be viewed naively. Unforgettably clear to the children is the realization that some things are not what they appear to be. This realization precedes the appreciation of the full nature of reality.

Professor Alfonso Ortiz, anthropologist and Tewa Indian, has pointed out that in the Pueblo worldview "all things are thought to have two aspects, essence and matter."[1] In the shadow cast by the destruction of their naiveté, the initiated children are made aware of the "essence" or sacrality of things they had until then seen only as "matter." Thus, the initiation serves to bring the children to the threshold of religious awareness and as a consequence initiates their religious lives. Once begun, the lifetime of the Hopi is a gradual progression in the acquisition of knowledge and the appreciation of the nature of "space, time, being and becoming," to use the subtitle of Ortiz's book The Tewa World.

This brings us back to the question of truth regarding the Hopi statement that when one dons the kachina mask he becomes a kachina. Given the appreciation by the initiated Hopi of the full nature of reality in both its material and essential aspects, the truth of the statement can be more clearly understood. By donning the kachina mask, a Hopi gives life and action to the mask, thus making the kachina essence present in material form. Mircea Eliade illuminates this point in his book *The Sacred and the Profane*: "by manifesting the sacred, any object becomes *something else*, yet it continues to remain itself." The anomaly we observe in the Hopi statement that he becomes a kachina is but an expression of the paradox of sacredness; but, in this case, the sacred object is the Hopi himself. By wearing the kachina mask, the Hopi manifests the sacred. He becomes the sacred kachina, yet continues to be himself. We, as uninitiated outsiders, observe only the material form. The spirit, or essence, of the kachina is present as well, but that can be perceived only by the initiated. The material presence without the spiritual is but mere impersonation—a dramatic performance, a work of art. The spiritual without the material remains unmanifest; it leaves no object for thought or speech or action. The spiritual must reside in some manifest form to be held in common by the community. The view, often taken, that the kachinas are "merely impersonations" fails to recognize the full religious nature of the kachina performances. It also fails to take into account the truth of the statement. If the kachinas are not present in both material and essential form, the events could scarcely be called religious.

Both Navajo and Hopi religions evidence an appreciation for the power of symbolization. Only through symbolization is the sacred manifest; the subtleties are many. On the one hand, the mundane materials which comprise religious symbols must never be taken as being more than the simple ordinary earthy elements they are. This fact is driven home in the disenchantment with the material appearance of the kachinas experienced by the children undergoing initiation. It is also evident in the example of the sandpainting rite from Navajo culture. On the other hand, the ordinary materials *when presented in the proper form* manifest the sacred. Both Navajo sandpaintings and Hopi kachinas have the power to order and affect the world in a very profound way.

I think that this deep appreciation for the process of the mani-festation of the sacred is broadly held among native Americans. One of the best formulations of it I know is found in the wisdom of the Oglala Sioux, Black Elk, as told to John Neihardt in *Black Elk Speaks*. As a youth, Black Elk was the recipient of a remarkable vision which he looked to as a guide throughout his life. For many years he kept the vision to himself, fearing to tell others. But as time went on, he found rising within him an even greater fear. Part of the message given him was that he was to enact the vision in ritual form for the people to see. This was a common practice among the Dakota. An old medicine man from whom Black Elk sought guidance warned him that if the vision were not performed, something very bad would happen to him.

Under Black Elk's direction, preparations were immediately be-gun so that the vision could be enacted by the people. Black Elk recalls how he experienced the enactment of his vision.

> I looked about me and could see that what we then were doing was like a shadow cast upon the earth from yonder vision in the heavens, so bright it was and clear. I knew the real was yonder and the darkened dream of it was here (173).

There is a sense in which the Navajo sandpaintings, the Hopi kachina masks, and many other native American ritual acts share the properties of a shadow of a vision yonder. I have stressed that it is the form more than the substance that is important in mani-festing the sacred forces of life. Certainly this is characteristic of shadows. Further, there is a "thinness" to ritual objects and acts which finds them to be real and meaningful only when cast in the light of "the yonder vision." This fragility is illustrated in the Navajo sandpaintings which are destroyed in the very acts by which they are of service. All of this is a constant reminder that the material symbols exist and are meaningful only in the degree to which they manifest the sacred. Were it not for these shadows cast by the vision yonder, American Indian religion would be confined to the experience of rarified mystical moments. The shadow may appear bright and clear as it did to Black Elk, or dark and foreboding as it does to Hopi kachina cult initiates, but the shadows integrate American Indian religion with a distinctive way of living and interpreting life.

5

On Seeing With the Eye
of the Native European

W. RICHARD COMSTOCK

We begin with a meeting between an "I" and a "thou" and a crucial mistake on both sides.

> At daybreak they saw an island full of green trees and abounding
> in springs . . . and inhabited by a multitude of people who hastened
> to the shore, astounded and marveling at the sight of the ships,
> which they took for animals. These people could hardly wait to see
> what sort of things the ships were. The Christians were no less
> eager to know what manner of people they had to do with.[1]

It was the morning of 12 October 1492 at San Salvador. This account of the first meeting between Columbus and his European crew with the native Americans is provided by Columbus's son Ferdinand. The passage is memorable for the depiction of high expectation on both sides. Each faces the "other." What is the "other" like?

The essays in this volume are devoted to seeing with the native American eye. But the act of "seeing" between human beings is a two-way affair. As each looks at the "other," he sees himself reflected and transformed by the image in the other's mind of what he is like.[2] Here in Ferdinand's account are the principle elements of the fatal misunderstanding and misapprehension that was to characterize the confrontation between native European and native American down to the present.

On one side, the natives made an error. According to Columbus: "They practice no kind of idolatry, but have a firm belief that all strength and power, and indeed, all good things, are in heaven and that I had descended from thence with these ships and sailors, and under this impression was I received after they had thrown aside their fears."[3] This mistake was in the end a fatal one for the native Americans. Perhaps it is inevitable that people possessing a more complex and powerful technology will appear as gods to those possessing a different technology with less potential for destructive acts. But in this case the "gods" possessing the superior technology had not achieved the mastery of themselves and the peace and impassibility of divinity; they rather were still driven by titanic energies that Zeus long ago had sought to control and by a restless Faustian ambition that God had not quelled.

Still, in the beginning the meeting seemed more charming than perilous. The natives made a childlike error. "They had no arms like ours, nor knew thereof; for when the Christians showed them a naked sword, they foolishly grasped it by the blade and cut themselves."[4] This act of misplaced trust was to occur again and again in the future on an ever larger scale and with ever more fatal consequences.

On the side of the "Christians," there was a sense of diminished expectations. The natives seemed to be more naive and simple than Columbus had been led to believe. However, there were advantages to the situation: "The Admiral, perceiving they were a gentle, peaceful, and very simply people, gave them little red caps and glass beads which they hung about their necks, together with other trifles that they cherished as if they were precious stones of great price."[5] Columbus proceeded to teach the natives his own tongue and his crew chose wives from among them. The future seemed big with promise, amicable relations, trade, the finding of gold, the penetration perhaps to an earthly paradise God had kept hidden until now.

For what exactly had Columbus discovered? From the moment that Columbus returned to Spain with the account of his successful voyage, informed opinion differed. The sphericity of the earth was no new theory spawned by Columbus for the first time. By the fourteenth century, scholars generally accepted Ptolemy's theory that the earth was round, but they also accepted a mapping of this world into three main continents—Europe, Asia, Africa.[6] As Leslie Fiedler points out, this was a world with a North, South, and East, along with a West that was closed.[7] By whom? Perhaps by God, who had placed the earthly paradise of Eden in the west and closed it off from man until the present days of a glorious new birth for mankind.

It is this consideration that accounts for the conflicting interpretations of what Columbus had accomplished, promulgated by Columbus himself and by many of his contemporaries, both friends and enemies. On the one hand, we have the well-known explanation suggested by Columbus that his feat was a paradoxical one. He had traveled west to reach the East. Whether sincerely or with the deceptive intention to increase interest and support for his enterprise, Columbus claimed to have reached the fabled but known East by a direct sea route. The native Americans were thereby bequeathed a name—"Indian"—which falsifies who they in fact are. Columbus felt the discrepancy. The first native Americans that he met clearly had a tribal technology different from that to be expected of an exotic Eastern civilization. As Samuel Morison puts it: "Columbus would rather have encountered sophisticated Orientals than "noble savages," but as usual he made the best of the situation."[8]

So another interpretation was suggested. Columbus had not reached the fabulous but mundane "East"; he had, rather, reached the sacred region of the original Paradise of man, before he fell into this world of sin and pain. In his letter to the sovereigns, Columbus suggests that while the earthly Paradise is in the "East," it is perhaps an island separated from the Asiatic mainland, and so in another sense is a new fourth continent of the world—the west.[9] Columbus wondered if the Orinoco River was actually the Gihon, one of the four rivers that, according to Genesis, flow out of Eden. In that case, he had reached, if not Paradise, then its outer proximity.[10]

What is important to our concern is that the factual reports about America and its native inhabitants were inevitably and for a variety of reasons intertwined with myth, theology, fantasy, and dreams. Columbus was a worldly man in that he was a seaman with a theory that proved to have practical consequences. He was also a leader who successfully commanded a voyage into unknown worlds together with a safe return. Yet his goal, while practical, was fraught with the weight of myth. And the importance of this ambiguous interweaving of mythic and worldly fact was that it caused the European to "see" the native American in certain contradictory ways that had fatal consequences. The very name "Indian" is indicative of this almost deliberate refusal of the European to see the native American in factual terms.

Even when the reality of the Americas as continents between Europe and Asia was established, the name "Indian" remained the appellation by which the native inhabitants continued to be designated. It was as if the European was refusing to see the native American as they were, but insisted on seeing them through the eyes of myth and legend. Names are important, and the resolute misnaming of entire tribes and clans of diverse peoples no doubt played a crucial role in the tragic destiny that was to befall the native American. As Scott Momaday observes: "A word has power in and of itself. It comes from nothing into sound and meaning. It gives origin to all things."[11] In naming the native Americans as they did, the European invaders created as much as they discovered the phenomenon that was the "Indian."

Paradise belongs to the "sacred" world of the gods, not the mundane world of secular men and women. If the native Americans were part of the sacred world, even if perhaps only on its outer boundaries, then they were beings either more or less than strictly human. They were gods or demons, unfallen creatures possessing an original innocence or devils with a brutish evil beyond human ken. In the early encounters of European settlers with native Americans, we see both images operating in the white man's imagination. To some Christians the native American appears as an unfallen creature close to God and either not needing salvation or else readily open to the healing Word of the Lord. To others he is a devil of such wickedness, cruelty, and lust that redemption is impossible.

Let us consider one striking example of this polar contrast to serve as a general paradigm. Frank Getlein makes the point in a memorable way through the rendering of the native American in pictorial art. *The Peaceable Kingdom* was painted by the American primitivist Edward Hicks, a Quaker preacher profoundly influenced by the famous treaties made by William Penn with the native Americans (1683–1750). Penn's achievement was a remarkable one, since the faithfulness with which he honored the treaty had created a spirit of good will that lasted fifty years. In *The Peaceable Kingdom*, Hicks presents the visionary and religious significance of what has happened. To the left and in the middle ground, Penn and his associates stand in noble posture as they make the treaty with a group of native Americans of equal nobility. Behind is the Delaware River, to which are added some imaginary mountains that contribute to the beauty and wonder of the scene. In the middle of the river is Penn's ship, a delicate and almost unearthly vessel. To the right and in the foreground, dominating the picture, is a literal rendering of the prophecy from Isaiah.

> The wolf also shall dwell with the lamb, and the leopard shall lie down with kid; and the calf and young lion and the fatling together; and a little child shall lead them (Isa. 11:6).

The animals in pairs as described by the prophet are assembled by Hicks together with two small children lying together in the middle, another child has each of his hands on one of the animals. The picture of Penn signing the treaty was copied from an already well-known painting by Benjamin West. The scene of the eschatological union of man and nature had been made many times before by Hicks himself. The fusion of the two into one painting enabled Hicks to communicate the millennial hope for final reconciliation amongst all aspects of God's creation. Animals, nature, Europeans, native Americans are transfigured together into a world of final supernal harmony.

By way of contrast, we may consider the painting entitled *The Death of Jane McCrea*, done in 1804 by John Vanderlyn. Vanderlyn was an American born on the eve of the American Revolution, but his esthetic goals were formed by European neoclassical ideals. While Hicks is the visionary primitive, Vanderlyn is the cultured artist aware of the distinction between civilization and its barbaric antithesis. So in *The Death of Jane McCrae* Vanderlyn depicts a true event that had been the subject of much controversy. The English general John Burgoyne (Gentleman Johnny) had enlisted the aid of "Indians" in his attempt to subdue the colonists. In the process, Jane McCrae had been scalped by the "Indians," though they claimed she had already been killed by a stray musket bullet at the battle of Fort Edward. Burgoyne, shocked at such treatment of a woman, had reprimanded the "Indians" with such severity that the alliance was dissolved. The event caused great indignation among the colonists, and many who had been neutral now flocked to the cause of rebellion against the crown. Burgoyne was defeated at Saratoga and returned to England, where he was denounced both for his defeat and for his attempt to use an uncivilized and barbaric people in a civilized cause.

With these events in mind, Vanderlyn presents us with a noble woman on one knee, her hand held by one "Indian" with a tomahawk in his other hand. A second "Indian" holds her hair and is about to kill and scalp her. Though the native figures have a rude grandeur to their bodies, their faces reveal an unrelenting savagery and brutality. Frank Getlein comments on these two pictures and observes:

> It is not too fanciful to imagine that both images of Indians are also projections by the immigrant Europeans of aspects of their own spiritual reality they are all too conscious of. Under the Puritan morality that came to dominate in the new Republic, the white Americans were on the one hand concerned to keep in check their own savagery, while on the other they yearned toward an imagined prelapsarian paradise, where equity and perfect justice governed all relationships. The Indian, a little too conveniently, came to represent both these opposing forces within the white American out to capture a continent while dreaming of perfect peace.[12]

We have here a striking example of the role of myth in human perception. Many thinkers see myth as a purely distorting medium that falsifies reality; others argue that it opens up the "truth" inherent in the merely factual surface of things.[13] Perhaps it is the case that myth and empirical fact operate in a kind of dialectic interaction which, when properly related, is productive of genuine insight; on the other hand, when the two are inadequately connected, distortion and misunderstanding ensue.

In the case of the native American, both the negative and positive functions of myth are in evidence. We cannot say that the mythic spectacles with which the European settler saw the native American were in all respects wrong, but the misalliance between the white man's dreams and his knowledge had unfortunate results for the native American's future. In this respect, the thought of Jean-Jacques Rousseau is important.

Rousseau is usually interpreted as the leading exponent of the sentimental view of the native American as the "noble savage" uncorrupted by civilization. In point of fact, Rousseau's argument is different, and if it had been properly understood, a more balanced equilibrium between myth and fact might have resulted. In his two famous *Discourses*, Rousseau uses the model of the uncivilized native as a kind of heuristic paradigm by which to expose the weakness of civilization. Nevertheless, he has no romantic illusions that the European either can or ought to return to some paradisiacal state untouched by civilization. Howover, if the man of a complex technological culture can perceive some of the virtues present in the native, Rousseau hopes that this can serve as a corrective against some of the unnecessary pitfalls into which Western man has been led by a civilized technology cut off completely from the lifestyle of tribal man.

Furthermore, Rousseau does not sentimentalize the native as if he were a vehicle of some universal unselfish love. Man in the state of nature does possess a natural pity or sympathy for others, but he also possesses a drive for self-survival.[14] Rousseau's point is that man in the state of nature is neither a brute seeking to pillage, rape, and destroy his neighbor, nor a saint concerned only with the other's welfare. To Rousseau the life of the natural man is not "nasty, brutish, short;" it is "simple, uniform, solitary;"[15] uncivilized man is neither a ravenous beast nor an angel. He is aware of his body, his natural needs, his love of freedom. He neither hates nor embraces his neighbor, but lives a life in which his openness to the natural processes of life provides him with health and a kind of robust corporeal tranquility.[16]

> Let us conclude that wandering in the forests, without industry, without speech, without domicile, without war and without liaisons, with no need of his fellowmen, likewise with no desire to harm them, perhaps never even recognizing any one individually, savage man, subject to few passions and self-sufficient, had only the sentiments and intellect suited to that state; he felt only his true needs, saw only what he believed he had an interest to see; and his intelligence made no more progress than his vanity.[17]

It is clear that this is no description of any actually existing primitive man or tribal society. It is what Max Weber later called an "ideal type." My point is only that Rousseau's image of the man of nature is a more productive one than either the paradisiacal god or unredeemable devil that has haunted the settler's imagination down to the present. This is not to deny that there is some idealization in Rousseau's image, but as one puts the elements of his picture together, it is surprisingly close to that provided by a more knowledgeable reporter like Scott Momaday. Momaday records the memories of his Kiowa ancestors in a way that conveys both the dignity and the hardness of their lives. They belong to no paradise of painless bliss. For example, Momaday writes:

> In the Kiowa calendar, there is graphic proof that the lives of women were hard, whether they were "bad women" or not. Only the captives, who were slaves, held lower status. During the Sun Dance of 1843, a man stabbed his wife in the breast because she accepted Chief Dohasan's invitation to ride with him in the ceremonial procession.[18]

But this "fact" does not mean the Kiowa are devils any more than that they are saints. To Momaday the Kiowa are native Americans, lovers of the earth, great warriors. My point is that Rousseau also saw this, and he emphasized not the sentimental love of the native but his essential dignity and his need for freedom.[19]

Some students of myth argue that often a transition can be traced in a culture from a focus on myth as stories of gods and supernatural beings to the world of the epic, where the figures are extraordinary but, nonetheless, human.[20] Such a transition can be traced in the history of the way the European settler has seen the native American. Omitting many details and stages in this transition, let us in this brief essay turn from the mythic perceptions we have described in the original meeting between native American and European invader to the climax of the story, when the white man has overcome an entire continent and completely subdued its native inhabitants. Now we find the victor perceiving his victim through the forms of epic and heroic action. The native Americans are no longer perceived as gods or devils. Subdued, defeated, they are transformed by the conquerors into tragic heroes. We now encounter the image of "the stoic warrior in noble defeat."

The factual history of the wars between native Americans and the white invaders is a very sordid one. There are incidents of noble action that can be cited on both sides; furthermore, accounts of atrocities from both camps are easily verified. But the overwhelming import of these wars is not one of two brave armies facing each other on an equal footing. Rather, we have here the story of a people with a superior technology and also superior numbers who more than defeat an enemy with fewer resources. *Defeat* is a word conveying connotations of epic nobility and grandeur that is in contrast to the ugly facts of a civilized people with superior technology destroying the "savage" enemy, decimating his numbers to a point approaching genocide, and who then completely destroy the spirit, the culture, the ethos of those who survive.[21]

But it is not my purpose to make a proper historical judgment about what actually happened, but rather to consider the dramatic image by which these events were perceived in the white man's imagination. As I have suggested, what occurred was the emergence of the image of the "stoic warrior in noble defeat."

The paradigm of this image is the well-known sculpture by James Earle Frazer in 1915 entitled "End of the Trail." Here, we see a noble Indian on his horse, the head of both horse and rider bowed and the lance in the warrior's right hand bent to the earth. The figure is defeated, but he is noble, grand, imparting an aura of tragic dignity. This figure has become a constituent part of the American national consciousness, because Earle Frazer also made for the United States government a model of this sculpture for the famous Indian Head nickel.[22]

Now, the intriguing point here is to consider the meaning of this image for the conqueror. The issue is not about the truth of the image. It is a fact that the native bearing in actuality does convey, a balance of courage, stoic impassibility, and silent serenity that has won the admiration of the white man. But why has the white man chosen to emphasize this quality at the very moment in history when he is relentlessly destroying the culture of which this demeanor is a significant manifestation? Is it not the case that if the white man can perceive himself as having vanquished a noble enemy, then he can understand himself also as a noble victor and not a cruel and heartless lord?

Thus, among many examples of the tragic disjunction between image and act, let us consider two. First is the story of Chief Joseph of the Nez Perces.[23] When Joseph refused the orders of the United States government to move his people from Wallowa Valley, General Howard was sent in 1877 with troops to enforce the edict. Joseph decided to lead his people to Canada. Through a series of brilliant maneuvers, Joseph for many months eluded the troops attempting to capture him but was finally trapped near the border between Montana and Canada. Defeated more by the severity of the winter than General Howard's troops, Joseph surrendered. His tribulations captured the imagination and admiration of white Americans and his speech of surrender was remembered for its dignity and eloquence.

> Tell General Howard I know his heart. What he told me before I have in my heart. I am tired of fighting. Our chiefs are killed. Looking Glass is dead. Toohoolhoolzote is dead. The old men are all dead. It is the young men who say yes or no. He who led on the young men (Ollokot) is dead. It is cold and we have no blankets. The little children are freezing to death. My people, some of them, have run away to the hills, and have no blankets, no food; no one knows where they are—perhaps freezing to death. I want to have time to look for my children and see how many of them I can find. Maybe I shall find them among the dead. Hear me, my chiefs! I am tired; my heart is sick and sad. From where the sun now stands I will fight no more forever.[24]

However, the admiration for Joseph as the "stoic warrior in noble defeat" did not prevent the government from shipping what remained of the tribe to Fort Leavenworth, Kansas. Joseph was not allowed to join his people but was forced to live out the remainder of his life at the Colville Reservation in Washington. Where he died in 1904.

Our second example concerns a similar event in the history of the Cheyenne. After their final defeat, various tribes of Cheyenne had been moved to Fort Reno, Oklahoma, almost a thousand miles from their former life on the Colorado and the Kansas Plains. Unhappy with their new situation, 297 men, women, and children decided to leave the reservation assigned to them and make the trek back to their original home. Their journey is another astonishing moment in the tragic demise of a great people.

In 1964, a movie entitled *Cheyenne Autumn*, directed by John Ford, was released. John Ford is noted for his innumerable westerns, most of them well crafted, many faithful to authentic details about the West, since Ford was extremely well read, almost an authority, on the history of the development of the West. However, his movies were, in the main, presented from the white man's point of view. The native Americans were savages on horses who attacked wagon trains and were shot down in droves by soldiers and settlers. One movie, *My Darling Clementine* (1946), an exceedingly well-made and well-received work, has an unfortunate scene that, however, may accurately convey the attitudes of the white man at the time. Wyatt Earp (played convincingly by Henry Fonda) finds the people of Tombstone frightened by a drunken Indian in a saloon. Earp easily disarms him, kicks him in the rump, and says with paternal severity: "Indian, get out of town and stay out." To the townspeople, he says with moral disgust: "What kind of town is this—selling whiskey to Indians?"[25]

Now in 1964, Ford had a different point of view. In a later interview, he declared:

> I had wanted to make it [*Cheyenne Autumn*] for a long time. I had killed more Indians than Custer, Beecher, and Chivington put together, and people in Europe always want to know about the Indians. There are two sides to every story, but I wanted to show their point of view for a change. Let's face it, we've treated them

very badly—it's a blot on our shield; we've cheated and robbed, killed, murdered, massacred and everything else, but they kill one white man and, God, out come the troops.[26]

It is interesting to see how Ford dealt with a story to be told from "their point of view for a change." The most moving and effective scene is the opening. The Cheyenne stand in the hot sun hour after hour, expecting the word from government officials that will be a positive response to their grievance. They stand in quiet stolid dignity, waiting for the answer that never comes. The camera moves from face to face. We see the courage, stoical indifference to pain, the patient demand for justice that is in each visage. Ford here provides us with an effective cinematic image of "the stoic warrior in noble defeat."

The rest of the movie is a disappointment so far as an unflinching openness to painful truth is concerned. According to history, about one hundred of the Cheyenne, after an arduous journey, were captured by soldiers and imprisoned in a barracks at Fort Robinson, Nebraska. When they refused orders to begin a suicidal march south in the dead of winter, Captain Wessells denied them food and water until they changed their minds. After five days of silent waiting, the Cheyenne suddenly burst out of the barracks, killed many soldiers, and escaped. They were pursued and recaptured. The various groups of wandering Cheyenne were eventually all rounded up and relocated in different reservations. Most had died, and those who remained alive were demoralized. It should be emphasized that of the original group of 297 persons, less than a third were warriors. The rest were women and children.

Ford's movie retells many of the incidents, but the indictment of the white man is softened, even sentimentalized. We feel that Captain Wessells (played by Karl Malden) is almost psychotic, completely misunderstanding the orders from Washington when he tries to force the imprisoned Cheyenne to make the suicidal journey. Furthermore, Wyatt Earp (this time played by James Stewart) is introduced to provide the focus of a comic interlude in the middle of the tragedy. The residents of Dodge City are convinced they will be massacred by the migrating Cheyenne. Someone fires a shot and the brave defenders run "like hell," to the disgust of Earp. However, in later engagements of the film, the scene was so mutilated that its point is lost and the presence of Earp seems a curious anomaly in the midst of the tragic story that is unfolding.

More important, the film assures us that Secretary of the Interior Carl Schurz (played by Edward G. Robinson) truly cares about the plight of the Cheyenne and all native Americans, but is frustrated by "politicians." Still, the film ends with Schurz personally meeting with the Cheyenne. He offers the chiefs one of his cigars instead of a peace pipe, to institute "a new custom." The film thus has an upbeat ending. Through tragic misunderstanding, the Cheyenne has unjustly suffered and endured his lot with stoic dignity. But now, understanding and justice is about to prevail. The disintegration and demoralization of the Cheyenne culture is muted. The white man has made his peace with "the stoic warrior in noble defeat."

What is missing, what perhaps the white can never provide, is the sense, the felt experience as actually lived, of what the defeat of the native American entailed. Here, the sparse clean prose of N. Scott Momaday is important. His Pulitzer-Prize–winning novel, *House Made of Dawn*, fulfills all the canons of the white man's standards of literary excellence, but the experience he conveys is that which only the native American has known. Although the novel is fiction, the reminiscences of the protagonist are based on historical events. The novel tells of the attempt of the Kiowa in 1890 to perform the Sun Dance.

> Before the dance could begin, a company of soldiers rode out from Fort Sill under orders to disperse the tribe. Forbidden without cause the essential act of their faith, having seen wild herds slaughtered and left to rot upon the ground, the Kiowas backed away forever from the tree. That was July 20, 1890, at the great bend of the Washita. My grandmother was there. Without bitterness, and for as long as she lived, she bore a vision of deicide.[27]

It is significant that the word *deicide* is here used. In the 1960s, there was much talk among white theologians about the "death of

God." Some claimed to be puzzled about what the phrase meant. Perhaps it is the experience of the native American that invests it with authentic meaning. Perhaps the "death of God" is the loss of a world and way of life of which technological man is only now beginning to be aware.

What are we to conclude from this tragic history? In my opinion, moral flagellation is too easy an answer. It is true that the white man has been cruel, heartless, unjust. Yet the issue is not really illuminated in the terms of individual or social morality. By citing individual examples, we can demonstrate both the generosity and the cruelty of the white man; but the same method will yield the same result if we consider the native American from this perspective also. It is not a question of the moral qualities of either peoples considered as individuals or as races. The real problem seems to be the difficulty in harmoniously relating different societal and economic modes of life. The peoples with advanced mechanical technologies—whatever their race—have been heartless in their treatment of societies based on a simpler technology and kinship social structures. It is as if the societies with complex technologies have felt some kind of threat from these people so easy to defeat in an uneven battle, but so difficult to exorcise from the secret imaginings of their hearts.

Lévi-Strauss points out that tribal societies everywhere are fast disappearing. There are now about 40,000 natives left in Australia, where at the beginning of this century, there were 250,000. Between 1900 and 1950, over ninety tribes have been wiped out in Brazil. During the same period, fifteen South American languages have ceased to be spoken.[28] The same, of course, is true of the native North American: Dee Brown quotes a Cheyenne warrior: "We will go North at all hazards and if we die in battle our names will be remembered and cherished by all our people." Observes Brown: "Soon there would be no one left to remember, no one to speak their names now that they were gone."[29]

Yet as the native American disappears from history, he reappears; we might almost say he erupts once again in the white man's imagination. The conqueror is not so sure he is the victor. His children begin to doubt the wisdom of the technological mind. It vanquishes its enemies and in the process seems to murder its own heart. Sons and daughters of the technological world wonder who they are. In their confusion they turn to the last vestiges of the culture their fathers murdered. They read the words of Black Elk. They learn of Hopi myths, the rituals of pain and ecstasy enacted in the sun dance of Sioux, Arapaho, and Cheyenne. Is there wisdom here desperately needed if the technological victor is not to destroy himself at the moment of his supposed triumph?

We do not know. We have only questions, nagging doubts, perplexities, mysteries. The act of imaging continues. Let us conclude with a striking example of where we are. In 1961, Ken Kesey finished writing his first novel, *One Flew Over the Cuckoo's Nest*. The novel tells of the adventures of R. P. McMurphy, a Dionysian Irishman who is admitted to a state mental institution. One source of the power of the novel lies in its vivid sketches of various inmates: Billie Bibbit, Mr. Harding, and also, of course, the striking portrait of the imposing head nurse, Miss Ratched. In 1961, Kesey had worked as an aide in Menlo VA Hospital, and these sketches were based on real people that he had met at that time, with one important exception.

Kesey had trouble getting his novel into shape until he hit upon a happy inspiration. He decided to present his story from the personal viewpoint of a completely demoralized, deeply psychotic "Indian" patient named Chief Broom. Although Broom is seven feet tall, he spends much of his time in the fetal position, is constantly terrified of Nurse Ratched and the hospital attendants. All the events are told through his distorted vision. As the novel progresses, Broom changes, develops courage, finds his identity. Having divested himself of his psychotic terrors, Broom, at the conclusion of the novel, assumes his true height and stature and leaves the institution. He plans to return to the place of his origin. The novel concludes with Broom's words: "I'd just like to look over the country around the gorge again, just to bring some of it clear in my mind again. I been away a long time."[30]

Kesey claims that once he chose to write the novel from Broom's perspective, his creative difficulties vanished and the novel was speedily completed. But if Kesey had the novelist's ability to transform real people into vivid fictional creations, on whom was Chief Broom based? The answer is astonishing. Kesey had no personal knowledge at that time of native American culture. Chief Broom is entirely a product of his power of imaging, of his imagination. The facts are so important to our theme that it will be useful to cite Kesey's own account in full. Kesey writes:

Which brings us to the last question: if real people and situations inspired the novel's secondary characters, and the longings of these people molded the hero, where then did the narrator come from? What inspired Chief Broom?

Peyote, I used to claim, inspired my Chief narrator, because it was after choking down eight of the little cactus plants that I wrote the first three pages. These pages remained almost completely unchanged through the numerous rewrites the book went through, and from this first spring I drew all the passion and perception the narrator spoke with during the ten month's writing that followed. That the narrator happened to be an Indian, despite my having never known an Indian before, I attributed to the well-known association between peyote and the certain tribes of our southwest: "The drug's reputation is bound to make one think of our red brothers," was how I used to explain it to admiring fans.

Now I don't think so.

After years of getting off behind being prognosticator of what seemed to me a stroke of genius, if not a masterstroke, I was notified that a certain spirit was getting a little peeved at the telegraph operator for being so presumptuous as to take credit for messages coming in, as though the receiver were sending the signal. "Mr. Bromden advises you cease speaking as his creator," I was notified; "Cease, or risk becoming prey to your own vain folly."

"Like how do you mean?" I wanted to know. "Being a genius is not something one gives up at the first idle threat . . ."

"Like if you keep thinking the Indian was your creation won't you eventually be forced to think of yourself as Tom Wolfe's creation?"

That was a point, I had to admit, but I still wasn't ready to relinquish a claim I was so fond of making, not just on the say-so of some nebulous notification.

"I'll believe it when I hear it from the horse's mouth."

As if I expected the big Indian to come to me in a dream, splendid and spectral in beads and buckskins, and proclaim:

"I . . . am the entity that spoke through your words. It was my task to acquaint your people with this particular transgression upon the human soul. You availed yourself of the transmission. If you need something of which to be proud, be proud of this availability.[31]

Clearly, something is happening to the consciousness of technological man that involves a continuing relation to the defeated native American antagonist. We do not know what the future holds. But that original meeting between native European and native American with which we began our essay is not yet over. Perhaps it has not yet really begun. The man of technology and the native American continue to look at each other. Each is not sure what he sees. The image of the "other" is formed into a shape, dissolved, reformed, transformed, ever growing, ever changing. Who is it that the man of technological civilization truly sees? Perhaps when he learns the answer to that question, he will also be able to answer that other question of his deepest perplexity. When he knows who the "other" is, perhaps he will know who he is too.

NOTES

1. Benjamin Keen, trans., *The Life of the Admiral Christopher Columbus by His Son Ferdinand* (New Jersey: Rutgers University Press, 1959), p. 59.
2. Erving Goffman, *Interaction Ritual* (New York: Doubleday and Co., 1967).

3. Letter to Rafael Sanchez, 14 March 1493, quoted in Wayne Moquin, ed., *Great Documents in American Indian History* (New York: Praeger Publishers, 1973), p. 3.

4. Keen, *The Life of the Admiral Christopher Columbus*, p. 61.

5. Ibid., p. 60. I am indebted to Leslie Fiedler for an appreciation of the symbolic importance of this event. *See* his *The Return of the Vanishing American* (New York: Stein and Day, 1969), pp. 36–41.

6. See map from the 1482 edition of the *Geographia* in David Divine, *The Opening of the World* (New York: C. P. Putnam's Sons, 1973), pp. 26–27.

7. Leslie A. Fiedler, *The Return of the Vanishing American* (New York: Stein and Day, 1969), pp. 36–37. Fiedler's account in turn is based on the fascinating account by Edmundo O'Gorman, *The Invention of America* (Bloomington: Indiana University Press, 1961). Cf. G. E. Nunn, *Geographical Conceptions of Columbus* (New York: American Geographical Society, 1924). Also Ernst and J. Lehner, *How They Saw the New World* (New York: Tudor Publishing, 1966), esp. chapter on "The Maps," pp. 31–74.

8. Samuel Eliot Morison, *Christopher Columbus, Mariner* (Boston: Little, Brown and Company, 1942, 1955), p. 52.

9. Bjorn Landstrom, *Columbus* (New York: The Macmillan Co., 1967), pp. 146–47.

10. See Mircea Eliade, *The Quest* (Chicago: University of Chicago Press, 1969), pp. 90–95; also George Williams, *Wilderness and Paradise in Christian Thought* (New York: Harper & Bros., 1962).

11. N. Scott Momaday, *The Way to Rainy Mountain* (New York: Ballantine Books, 1969), p. 42.

12. Frank Getlein, *The Lure of the Great West* (Wisconsin: Country Beautiful, 1973) p. 27.

13. Cf. Roland Barthes, *Mythologiques* (New York: Hill and Wang, 1957) with Mircea Eliade, *Myth and Reality* (New York: Harper and Row, 1963).

14. Jean-Jacques Rousseau, *The First and Second Discourses*, translated by Roger D. and Judith R. Masters (New York: St. Martin's Press, 1964) p. 150.

15. Ibid., p. 110.

16. Ibid., pp. 112–13.

17. Ibid, p. 137.

18. Momaday, *The Way to Rainy Mountain*, p. 79.

19. Rousseau, *The First and Second Discourses*, pp. 164–65, 224.

20. Northrop Frye, *Anatomy of Criticism* (Princeton: Princeton University Press, 1957).

21. Dee Brown, *Bury My Heart at Wounded Knee* (New York: Bantam Books, 1972).

22. Getlein, *The Lure of the Great West*, pp. 350–51. *Also* cf. the picture by Joseph Sharp entitled, significantly, "The Stoic," p. 323.

23. Recounted in Dee Brown, *Bury My Heart at Wounded Knee*, chapter 13. Also see the novel about Chief Joseph by James Foreman, *People of the Dream* (New York: Dell Publishing Co., 1972).
24. Brown, *Bury My Heart*, p. 312. Also see *Touch the Earth* compiled by T. C. McLuhan for moving examples of the eloquence of native Americans in defeat.
25. Philip French, *Westerns* (New York: The Viking Press, 1974), p. 87.
26. Quoted in Peter Bogdanovich, *John Ford* (Berkeley: University of California Press, 1968), p. 104.
27. N. Scott Momaday, *House Made of Dawn* (New York: New American Library, 1968), p. 122. Cf. his *The Way to Rainy Mountain*, p. 11.
28. Lévi-Strauss, "The Disappearance of Man," *New York Review of Books* 7, no. 1 (28 July 1966), pp. 6
29. Brown, *Bury My Heart*, p. 331.
30. Ken Kesey, *One Flew Over the Cuckoo's Nest*, test and criticism edition by John C. Pratt (New York: The Viking Press, 1973), p. 311.
31. Ken Kesey, *Kesey's Garage Sale* (New York: The Viking Press, 1973), pp. 14–15.

6

Native American Attitudes
to the Environment

N. SCOTT MOMADAY

The first thing to say about the native American perspective on environmental ethics is that there is a great deal to be said. I don't think that anyone has clearly understood yet how the Indian con-conceives of himself in relation to the landscape. We have formulated certain generalities about that relationship, and the generalities have served a purpose, but they have been rather too general. For example, take the idea that the Indian reveres the earth, thinks of it as the place of his origin and thinks of the sky also in a personal way. These statements are true. But they can also be misleading because they don't indicate anything about the nature of the relationship which is, I think, an intricate thing in itself.

I have done much thinking about the "Indian worldview," as it is sometimes called. And I have had some personal experience of Indian religion and Indian societies within the framework of a worldview. Sometime ago I wrote an essay entitled "An American

Note: This paper was adapted from transcriptions of oral remarks Professor Momaday made on this subject, informally, during a discussion with faculty and students.

Land Ethic" in which I tried to talk in certain ways about this idea of a native American attitude toward the landscape. And in that essay I made certain observations. I tried to express the notion first that the native American ethic with respect to the physical world is a matter of reciprocal appropriation: appropriations in which man invests himself in the landscape, and at the same time incorporates the landscape into his own most fundamental experience. That suggests a dichotomy, or a paradox, and I think it is a paradox. It is difficult to understand a relationship which is defined in these terms, and yet I don't know how better to define it.

Secondly, this appropriation is primarily a matter of the imagination. The appropriation is realized through an act of the imagination which is moral and kind. I mean to say that we are all, I suppose, at the most fundamental level what we imagine ourselves to be. And this is certainly true of the American Indian. If you want a definition, you would not go, I hope, to the stereotype which has burdened the American Indian for many years. He is not that befeathered spectacle who is always chasing John Wayne across the silver screen. Rather, he is someone who thinks of himself in a particular way and his idea comprehends his relationship to the physical world, among other things. He imagines himself in terms of that relationship and others. And it is that act of the imagination, that moral act of the imagination, which I think constitutes his understanding of the physical world.

Thirdly, this imagining, this understanding of the relationship between man and the landscape, or man and the physical world, man and nature, proceeds from a racial or cultural experience. I think his attitude toward the landscape has been formulated over a long period of time, and the length of time itself suggests an evolutionary process perhaps instead of a purely rational and decisive experience. Now I am not sure that you can understand me on this point; perhaps I should elaborate. I mean that the Indian has determined himself in his imagination over a period of untold generations. His racial memory is an essential part of his understanding. He understands himself more clearly than perhaps other people, given his situation in time and space. His heritage has always been rather closely focused, centered upon the landscape as a particular reality. Beyond this, the native American has a particular investment in vision and in the idea of vision. You are familiar with the term "vision quest" for example. This is another essential idea to the Indian worldview, particularly that view as it is expressed among the cultures of the Plains Indians. This is significant. I think we should not lose the force of the idea of seeing something or envisioning something in a particular way. I happen to think that there are two visions in particular with reference to man and his relationship to the natural world. One is physical and the other is imaginative. And we all deal in one way or another with these visions simultaneously. If I can try to find an analogy, it's rather like looking through the viewfinder of a camera, the viewfinder which is based upon the principle of the split image. And it is a matter of trying to align the two planes of that particular view. This can be used as an example of how we look at the world around us. We see it with the physical eye. We see it as it appears to us, in one dimension of reality. But we also see it with the eye of the mind. It seems to me that the Indian has achieved a particularly effective alignment of those two planes of vision. He perceives the landscape in both ways. He realizes a whole image from the possibilities within his reach. The moral implications of this are very far-reaching. Here is where we get into the consideration of religion and religious ideas and ideals.

There is another way in which I think one can very profitably and accurately think of the Indian in relation to the landscape and in terms of his idea of that relationship. This is to center on such a word as *appropriate*. The idea of "appropriateness" is central to the Indian experience of the natural world. It is a fundamental idea within his philosophy. I recall the story told to me some years ago by a friend, who is not himself a Navajo, but was married for a time to a Navajo girl and lived with her family in Southern Utah. And he said that he had been told this story and was passing it on to me. There was a man living in a remote place on the Navajo reservation who had lost his job and was having a difficult time making ends meet. He had a wife and several children. As a matter of fact, his wife was expecting another child. One day a friend came to visit him and perceived that his situation was bad. The friend said to him "Look, I see that you're in tight straits, I see you have many mouths to feed, that you have no wood and that there is very little food in your larder. But one thing puzzles me. I know you're a hunter, and I know, too, there are deer in the mountains very close at hand. Tell me, why don't you kill a deer so that you and your family might have fresh meat to eat?" And after a time the man replied, "No, it is inappropriate that I should take life just now when I am expecting the gift of life."

The implications of that idea, and the way in which the concept of appropriateness lies at the center of that little parable is a central consideration within the Indian world. You cannot understand how the Indian thinks of himself in relation to the world around him unless you understand his conception of what is appropriate; particularly what is morally appropriate within the context of that relationship.

QUESTION: Could you probe a little deeper into what lies behind the idea of appropriate or inappropriate behavior regarding the natural world. Is it a religious element? Is it biological or a matter of survival? How would you characterize what makes an action appropriate or inappropriate?

MOMADAY: It is certainly a fair question but I'm not sure that I have the answer to it. I suspect that whatever it is that makes for the idea of appropriateness is a very complex thing in itself. Many things constitute the idea of appropriateness. Basically, I think it is a moral idea as opposed to a religious one. It is a basic understanding of right within the framework of relationships, and, within the framework of that relationship I was talking about a moment ago, between man and the physical world. That which is appropriate within this context is that which is *natural*. This another key word. My father used to tell me of an old man who has lived a whole life. I have often thought of this image. The old man used to come to my grandfather's house periodically to pay visits, and my father has very vivid recollections of this man whom I never knew. But his name was Chaney. Father says that Chaney would come to the house and he would make himself perfectly at home. He would be passing by going from one place to another, exercising his ethnic prerogative for nomadism. But he would make my grandfather's house a kind of resting place. He stayed there on many occasions. My father says that every morning when Chaney was there as a guest he would get up in the first light, paint his face, go outside, face the east, and bring the sun out of the horizon. Then he would pray. He would pray aloud to the rising sun. He did that because it was appropriate that he should do that. He understood. Or perhaps I should say that in terms of his own understanding, the sun was the origin of his strength. He understood the sun, within a more formal religious context, similar to the way someone else understands the presence of a deity. And in the face of that recognition, he acted naturally or appropriately. Through the medium of prayer, he returned some of his strength to the sun. He did this everyday. It was a part of his daily life. It was as natural and appropriate to him as anything could be. There is in the Indian worldview this kind of understanding of what is and what is not appropriate. It isn't a matter of intellection. It is respect for the understanding of one's heritage. It is a kind of racial memory and it has its origin beyond any sort of historical experience. It reaches back to the dawn of time.

QUESTION: When talking about vision, you said that the Indians saw things physically and also with the eye of the mind, I think this is the way you put it. You also said that this was a whole image, and that it had certain moral implications. Would you elaborate further?

MOMADAY: I think there are different ways of seeing things. I myself am particularly interested in literature, and in the traditions of various peoples, the Indians in particular. I understand something of how this works within the context of literature. For example, in the nineteenth century in America, there were poets who were trying very hard to see nature and to write about it. This is one kind of vision. They succeeded in different ways, some succeeding more than others. They succeeded in seeing what was really there on the vision plain of the natural world and they translated that vision, or that perception of the natural world, into poetry. Many of them had a kind of scientific training. Their observations were trained through the study of botany, astronomy, or zoology, etc. This refers, of course, to one kind of vision.

But, obviously, this is not the sort of view of the landscape which characterizes the Indian world. His view rather is of a different and more imaginative kind. It is a more comprehensive view. When the native American looks at nature, it isn't with the idea of training a glass upon it, or pushing it away so that he can focus upon it from a distance. In his mind, nature is not something apart from him. He conceives of it, rather, as an element in which he exists. He has existence within that element, much in the same way we think of having existence within the element of air. It would be unimaginable for him to think of it in the way the nineteenth century "nature poets" thought of looking at nature and writing about it. They employed a kind of "esthetic distance," as it is sometimes called. This idea would be alien to the Indian. This is what I meant by trying to make the distinction between two sides of a split image.

QUESTION: So then, presumably in moral terms, the Indian would say that a person should not harm nature because it's something in which one participates oneself.

MOMADAY: This is one aspect of it. There is this moral aspect, and it refers to perfect alignment. The appropriation of both images into the one reality is what the Indian is concerned to do: to see what is really there, but also to see what is *really* there. This reminds me of another story. It is very brief. It was told to me by the same fellow who told me about the man who did not kill the deer. (To take a certain liberty with the title of a novel that

I know well.) He told me that while he himself was living in southern Utah with his wife's family, he became very ill. He contracted pneumonia. There was no doctor, no physician nearby. But there was a medicine man close at hand. The family called in a diagnostician (the traditional thing to do), who came and said that my friend was suffering from a particular malady whose cure would be the red-ant ceremony. So a man who is very well versed in that ceremony, a seer, a kind of specialist in the red-ant ceremony, came in and administered it to my friend. Soon after that my friend recovered completely. Not long after this he was talking to his father-in-law, and he was very curious about what had taken place. He said, "I wonder about the red-ant ceremony. Why is it that the diagnostician prescribed that particular ceremony for me?" His father-in-law looked at him and said, "Well, it was obvious to him that there were red ants in your system, and so we had to call in a seer to take the red ants out of your system." At this point, my friend became very incredulous, and said, "Yes, but surely you don't mean that there were red ants inside of me." His father-in-law looked at him for a moment, then said, "Not ants, but ants." Unless you understand this distinction, you might have difficulty understanding something about the Indian view of the natural world.

7

The Contribution of the Study of North American Indian Religions to the History of Religions

ÅKE HULTKRANTZ

Introduction

Some years ago a leading American authority in the field of religion, Professor Wilfred Cantwell Smith, remarked in a provocative article that the study of non-Christian religions should be entirely dedicated to the great contemporaneous traditions, Islam, Hinduism, Buddhism and so forth. In his estimation the religions of smaller ethnic groups should be omitted, and he praised those textbooks which avoid tribal religions in favor of a more exhaustive treatment of the living world religions. The motivation for this reasoning was simple enough: tribal religions were judged as crude remnants of past religious traditions which have no importance for the world of today. Nor could the study of these religions increase our understanding of the "we/they orientation" which is, according to Smith, of supreme interest to modern religionists. Moreover, Smith's demand that any statement about a religion should be approved by its devotees could not be satisfied if it originated from representatives of a tribal religion.[1]

It is perfectly clear that this position, if accepted, implies that the study of aboriginal North American religions should be of no concern to the historian of religion. These religions may be labeled tribal, or "primitive"—that is, molded in a formerly primitive technological milieu.[2] They are only embraced by small minorities of people, and they play an insignificant role in the world at large. It is, on the other hand, less conspicuous why their adherents would not lend themselves to a we/they interpretation. (I wish Dr. Smith could have listened to my discussions with a Shoshoni medicine man on the validity of religious beliefs.) It is furthermore enigmatic why they could not communicate in terms of the researcher's way of dealing with their religion—if this should prove necessary.[3] Smith's views remind us of those American anthropologists who discard the study of tribal societies as romantic antiquarianism and speak in favor of more research on modern complex civilizations.[4] Perhaps we can discern the American drive for more "practical" research, an extroverted outlook on the world, behind the screen of similar pronouncements.

This indifference to studies of tribal religions has also been obvious in European history of religions until recent times. As may emerge from a perusal of readers and textbooks in the discipline, for a long time the material and ideas have been taken primarily from the so-called civilizations (or the old high cultures in the Near East, India, and China, and their successors) as well as from the cosmopolitan cultures that were the cradles of the present great world religions. These religions are of course of utmost importance, but they constitute a part of the many religions which, in different places and at different times, have accompanied humanity. Any phenomenology of religion which does not take into closer account religious forms among preliterate peoples gives a false picture of the religious world. Fortunately, however, the widening world scene in our time has more and more aroused scientific interest in some of these neglected religions, in particular, African religions and modern syncretistic religions built up on the ruins of tribal religion. There is the prospect that in the future, and contrary to the opinion exposed at the beginning of this paper, historians of religions will come increasingly to observe the "primitive religions" in their multi-formity.

In this perspective, the North American Indian religions, which vary so drastically in quality, deserve a wider attention. For a long time they have been the almost exclusive hunting ground of American anthropologists. Certainly, American anthropologists have contributed many fine insights to our store of religious knowledge. We are reminded specifically of Boas's analyses of Kwakiutl religions, Lowie's and Radin's influential papers on Crow and Winnebago religions, Fletcher's investigations into Teton Dakota, Omaha and Pawnee religions, Hewitt's penetration of Iroquois religious ideas, Benedict's survey of guardian-spirit conceptions, Hallowell's presentation of the bear cult, and others.[5] However, all of these contributions belong to the first decades of our century. Later anthropologists have been less occupied with American Indian religion and, if they have dealt with religion at all, they have often done it with a sociological or psychoanalytic bias. It is important therefore that historians of religion, with their interest in religion *in et per se*, step in on the scene. Together with a new generation of anthropologists they may open new vistas on American Indian religions.

Until now North America has been a field for extra trips of historians of religion who have been specialists in other subjects. Pettazzoni, who wrote books and articles on North American mythology and particularly the trickster figure, was first a prominent classic scholar.[6] E. O. James, who composed an article on animistic beliefs in North America, is a learned compiler of European religions of the past, and a general phenomenologist.[7] Eliade, also a well-known phenomenologist of religion, and a good Indologist, has treated American shamanism in a famous monograph.[8] Bianchi, authority on Gnosticism, has included a chapter on the North American trickster and culture hero in a study of dualism.[9] This has been the pattern. What is needed, however, is full-time specialists on North American religions. They may call themselves anthropologists or historians. (In Europe historians of religion refer to themselves as anthropologists, or are trained in both subjects). Regardless of nomenclature, the important thing is that they concentrate their attention to North American Indian religion and orientate their descriptions and analyses around the form and content of religion. There are at present several researchers in both America and Europe who seem to turn in on this track. (Some of them will be mentioned later on.) Their task is both interesting and rewarding. North American religion cannot be considered a marginal area in religious studies any longer. Aboriginal North America is and has been the home of hundreds of religions which are interesting in themselves and have importance for the knowledge of religious expressions. It seems that the new research on these religions should be correlated with the early twentieth-century phase, when the theories and methods of religious studies were stimulated by the research focusing on North American Indians.

The renewed interest in North American aboriginal religion has several sources, beside the general concern for peoples outside the Euro-American sphere and the observation of new hybrid religious forms in these areas. One is the reawakening of the Indians themselves to new national consciousness, or supernational feelings—called pan-Indianism. They have shown us how a traditional religion can constitute a focus of ethnic identity, and an intertribal Peyote ritual can create a bond of commonness and unity between separate tribes. Another source is the growing realization among educated people that in many respects these religions attain a loftiness and a dignity that even surpass that of some of the supposed "higher" religions. The high-god concept and the beautiful symbolism bear witness to this. Finally, the modern concern with ecological problems invites us to a closer observation of the Indians on the religioecological level: the harmonious combination of nature and religion that they have achieved impresses every outsider. They evidence in their way of living and in their religion that human beings have to live with nature, and not against it, as is the case in our modern technocratic societies.

Let us now take a closer look at the contributions that the present research on North American religion has made to the history of religions, and also discuss some contributions which may be forth-coming.

Research on Traditional Religion

A major task of modern research will be to supply more knowledge on traditional religious forms in aboriginal North America, with the clear intention of making this area one of the great and well-known provinces in the history of religions. In Joseph Brown's words, we shall "give to the American Indian heritage its rightful place among the great spiritual traditions of mankind."[10]

Now, in anthropological circles it has long been considered that this work has been done and is finished. For instance, the research on Plains Indians and their religions had its high time in the begin-ning of this century, during the days when Dorsey, Wissler, Kroeber, Lowie, Grinnel and other field ethnographers were active here. Their ethnography was a "salvage ethnography," saving the rem-nants of old Plains religions and often building ritual reconstructions on hearsay and oral tradition. So it is undoubtedly true that such work has belonged to the past. Nevertheless, two things are for-gotten in this connection. First, the traditional religions live on, sometimes have even been invigorated. For instance, the Sun Dance has returned in places where it had dropped out as a consequence of the government's prohibition (now repealed) against it. Indeed, lately the Sun Dance has spread to tribes who either have not had it before or, as among the Crow, had lost their old form of Sun Dance.[11] Dusenberry has coined the term "persistence" to describe this force of nativism and traditionalism which makes the old religion the core of ethnic existence.[12] Second, the ethnographical sources compiled by Wissler *et consortes* often reveal an irritating barrenness when it comes to descriptions and analyses of religion. For instance, the Sun Dance is treated as a ritual complex where the religious motivation and symbolism is disregarded.[13] In other words, the most important aspects of the ceremony have been over-looked.

Facts like these encourage us to pursue two lines of research on Plains religions: first, continued field investigations, and second, further comparative analyses of existing documents. Both procedures complement each other. The field investigations provide us with new religious materials, and may help to clarify old issues and earlier unclear information. The comparative analyses may reveal to us living religion behind the sterile facts of ethnographical publications, and thus fertilize and stimulate the field investigations. It goes without saying that the engagement of educated Indians in both approaches would give the work increased value.

There are some modern publications which testify to the new interest in field investigations of Plains Indian religions. Gros Ventre religion has been covered in a volume by the late Father John Cooper;[14] aspects of Arapaho religion were published by Sister Inez Hilger;[15] and the main tribal mysteries of the Cheyenne Indians have been described in a beautiful work by Father Peter Powell.[16] Dusenberry's monograph on Plains Cree religion has already been mentioned. The Siouan religions have been studied quite intensely. Alfred Bowers has disclosed the religious and ceremonial organization of the Mandan and Hidatsa.[17] The great ceremony of the Mandan has won further attention by Ewers's republication, in a lavishly illustrated volume, of Catlin's famous O-kee-pa from 1867.[18] Joseph Brown's book The Sacred Pipe is perhaps at present the most widely read work on Plains Indian religion. It contains excellent materials on Oglala Dakota rites and beliefs dictated to Brown by Black Elk, the most renowned of Dakota medicine men in later times.[19] Brown is now preparing an analysis of Oglala religion built upon his field experience.[20]

It is significant that comparative analyses of ethnographical records from the Plains area, for the most part, have been undertaken by European Americanists. The reasons are obvious: they have fewer opportunities to conduct field research in America, and are therefore often forced to fall back upon literary sources. Besides, at least on the continent, their research traditions guide them to comparative library research. These works fall in two categories: regional monographs and thematic investigations. To the former belongs the thoughtful study of the religions of the Sioux tribes by Werner Müller (a good example of where symbolistic studies can lead us).[21] To the same range of studies may also be counted several small but important articles, such as Ewers's description of the Assiniboin bear cult on the northern Plains,[22] Dräger's analyses of Sun Dance paintings[23] and Hartmann's discussion of the Gros Ventre high-god concept.[24] Hultkrantz's survey of Plains-Prairie religion may also be included here.[25] Among the thematic investigations may be mentioned some recent studies of visionary and guardian-spirit experiences which indeed testify to a renewed interest in a field earlier analyzed by Wissler, Lowie, Benedict, and Blumensohn. Here belongs Coale's study of the guardian-spirit ideas among a tribe with a late influx of Plains-culture characteristics, the Nez Perce,[26] Arbman's exhaustive survey of fasting experiences in their connections with theory on ecstasy,[27] and Albers's and Parker's analysis of the relations between visionary experiences and sociopolitical structures on the Plains.[28] Closely related to these studies are a couple of new investigations of the Spirit Lodge, or Shaking Tent, a shamanistic ceremony.[29] Other thematic research enterprises comprise Lindig's comparative monograph on Omaha and Iroquois societies: secret societies, age societies, military societies in their religious and historical aspects,[30] and Hultkrantz's comparisons of Shoshoni and Dakota high-god concepts.[31]

This short and certainly not complete survey of present activities in the field of Plains-Indian religion could easily be supplemented with similar surveys of other North American Indian religious areas, such as the Southwest, the Plateau, the Eastern Woodlands, and so on. The last years have seen publications of such importance as a new treatise on Havasupai religion and mythology,[32] Codere's edition of Boas's manuscripts on Kwakiutl religion[33] and an assortment of new interpretations of the Great Medicine Society among the Central Algonkian and Northeastern Siouan tribes.[34] This work clearly demonstrates that research on traditional Indian religion is no finished chapter but, on the contrary, a living current activity. We recognize not only that fieldwork and comparative literary research continue, but that they have gained a distinctive depth and qualitative intensification.

No doubt the collaboration of students of religion in these tasks has meant the introduction of new angles of scientific exploration in Americanistic studies. As distinct from most anthropological studies, emphasis has been placed on religion as such. Whereas too many anthropologists view religion as a mere mechanism for providing social and cultural values (cf. Hultkrantz 1970 a), historians of religions tend healthily to regard religion as a means in itself, as the adequate instrument of *homo religiosus*. In this connection we should be aware of the functionalistic fallacy as first discussed by Gellner and expounded for religionists by Penner: the use and function of a religious phenomenon is not the same as its explanation and meaning.[35] The reductionist theory has to be abolished if we shall be able to arrive at a real understanding of American Indian religion as a value system and symbolic structure.

Phenomenological Research

The intensified research on North American Indian religions opens new vistas not only for our understanding of these religions in their ethnographical frame but also for our general understanding of religious forms. The results gained by Americanists may provide correctives to the phenomenological perspectives on religion. Until recently these perspectives have been largely molded by the impressions and experiences the authors of phenomenological works have had from studies of the religions of the civilizations.

It is unnecessary here to point out what stimulation the phenomenology of religion once received from the discovery and discussions of concepts like *orenda*, *manitou*, and *waḳanda*, or the elucidation of totemistic ideas, guardian spirit notions and high-god conceptions with the *creatio ex nihilo* motif, or the differentiation between shamanistic thinking and layman thinking, between the devoted religious persons and the "intermittently religious" (Radin). Indeed, some Indian concepts became the point of departure for new terms in the history of religions, just as once *totemism* had been formed from the Algonkian *totam*. Thus, scholars like Pfister and von Sydow used the term *orendism* (from Iroquois *orenda*) to denote the belief in impersonal power, also labeled *dynamism*; and Ankermann found the word *manituism* (from Algonkian *manitou*) a fitting term for the belief in guardian spirits, also called *individual totemism*.[36] However, during the last fifty years phenomenology of religion has gained more insights from the studies of the so-called high religions. One historian of religions has expressed the matter thus that for him issues like impersonal power, taboo, and soul beliefs have been left behind, or replaced by concepts like myth and rite, sacral kingship and high-god beliefs. All of these concepts are relevant to the Near Eastern religions.[37]

And yet, North American Indian religions have even more to offer to the phenomenologist. It may be, as Müller considers, that some of the old formulations from the study of American and other primitive religions were "desiccated" and less rewarding.[38] The modern contribution of Americanistic studies to the phenomenology of religion has less to deal with new concepts and new terms than with new contents and new dimensions. It is a well-known fact that a specialist in a certain religion tries to see all other religions in the light of his own findings. It is therefore important that phenomenology of religion, now largely imbued with the particular insights of Orientalists, is complemented with the specific experiences of Americanists. Indeed, some of the current concepts of the history of religions—like the formulation of the connections between myth and rite, or the dimensions of the high-god concept—would have to be changed in most textbooks if they were compared with the interpretations of North American Indian materials.

On this point I shall restrict myself to adduce my own reactions as an Americanist, not because I consider my own work among

North American Indians to be any way more important than that of my colleague Americanists, but because it is easier to judge the phenomenological approaches against the background of one's own results in the field. I should like to enumerate the following topics in the phenomenology of religion as being in need of revision in view of my findings:

1. *The importance of self-sacrifice, mutilation, and sufferings as means of creating a bond with the supernatural powers.* Although the "blood sacrifice complex," to quote Loeb,[39] has a restricted distribution among hunters and gatherers it expresses an attitude that has its counterpart in these cultures and probably also underlies such cosmogonic tales as Jensen's *Hainuwele* or immolation myth.[40] Man's greatest gift is to offer himself, under pain. Plains Indians are aware of the deep connection between such rituals and the crucifixion of Christ.

2. *The cosmic symbolism of rituals.* North American ceremonialism is sometimes dismissed with phrases like "repetitive," or "complicated without meaning." In actual fact, however, it reflects an intricate cosmic symbolism, and every move has its own import within the symbolic pattern. The realization of symbolic structure sheds light on the meaning of ceremonies. It is therefore desirable that this aspect of rituals will be observed more in the phenomenology of religions.

3. *The symbolism of ritual objects.* The straightforward praying to a cultic image is less frequent in aboriginal North America. For instance, prayers are given in connection with the opening of a medicine bag, or tribal bundle, but they are not directed to the bundle as such: they are directed to the supernatural powers which it represents. Medicine objects are no *Abgötter*. The venerative attitude, without real cult of the sacred object, is worth observing and should be recorded in phenomenological manuals.

4. *The fundamental importance of "animalism"—the conception of supernatural powers in animal forms—in precivilized societies.* In North American hunting cultures the supernatural beings express

themselves predominantly in animal disguise, and the animals are symbolically related to the supernatural world.[41] The supernatural master of animals, in particular, plays an important role.[42] Here is a concept of world-wide distribution that deserves fuller treatment in the phenomenology of religion. The importance of what Findeisen called "the animal stratum" (*Tierschicht*) for the development of religious ideas cannot on the whole be neglected.[43]

5. *The idea of the culture hero.* In spite of the fact that Breysig called attention to the culture hero (*Heilbringer*) some seventy years ago, this figure is seldom introduced in phenomenological works on religion. Where he appears authors are often confused as to his functions and general import. The typical culture-hero concepts belong to Africa, Oceania, and North America, but aspects of the idea are also met elsewhere, for instance, in Greek and Scandinavian religions. The North American data are eminently suited to outline the most characteristic features of the culture hero: his appearance in mythology (primarily), his trickster aspect, his opposition to the Creator, his possible relations to the master of the animals, etc.

6. *The nature of the high god.* On the whole, historians of religion have been too rigorous in discriminating between the Supreme Being and other divine beings. Thus they have created a gap between monotheism and polytheism. The facts do not speak in favor of this interpretation. Although developed forms of monotheism or polytheism occur in the high civilizations, the incipient form of theism includes both unity (one god) and pluralism (a host of divinities and spirits), depending upon the situation of beliefs or dominant patterns of thought.[44]

7. *The independent nature of the myth.* The majority of historians of religions seem to consider that myths complement cults and beliefs to make up an integrated picture of religion, and that myths are cultic texts. (This is the opinion at least, of the British and Scandinavian myth-and-ritual schools.) I challenge both these interpretations, if they claim to cover all the mythic material. It is true that myths *may* complement cults and beliefs, that they *may*

be cultic texts; but the North American mythologies also tell us that myth and religion may be separate entities. Sometimes they appear as segments of belief that almost exclude each other.[45]

Historical Research

The last hundred years has seen an immense accumulation of documents relating to North American Indians. Together with older materials—traveling accounts, government reports, missionary documents, etc.—they constitute excellent source material for the reconstruction of historical events and historical sequences within the field of religion. First of all, such reconstructions sharpen our knowledge of what actually happened in North American Indian religious history. Secondly, they give the general historian of religion a distinct idea of how religious processes have taken form in preliterary milieus in the past—a good substitution for the guesswork that took place in the old evolutionistic era and that occurs even today, here and there, in professional circles. Thirdly, despite the lack of pre-Columbian documents, the material at hand is sufficient to allow us to establish distributional series and chronological sequences which have importance for the general study of religions. North American religions can be linked historically to religious phenomena and patterns not only in Siberia but in the world at large.

The reconstruction of North American Indian religious history has three major roads to follow.

1. Reconstruction through analysis of archaelogical materials. A good example is offered in Howard's recent presentation of the "Southern Death Cult" in the prehistoric Mississippian-Southeastern region.[46]

2. Reconstruction through studies of documents from the historical era. A model for such research may be found in Fenton's classical volume on the character and distribution of the Calumet ceremonies and the Iroquois Eagle Dance.[47]

3. Reconstruction through oral testimony from Indian informants. This method once relied upon by such a distinguished anthro-

pologist as John Swanton was later discarded by Lowie, Steward, and other authorities.[48] Recently, however, students like Euler, Pendergast, and Meighan have reassessed the reliability of oral information.[49] It is apparently possible to trust Indian memory for three generations back in time. Together with documentary materials, oral testimony may supply reliable information for a longer span of time. We have examples of this in the reconstructions that have been made of the succession of keepers of tribal *palladia* among Plains Indian tribes: the keepers of the Kiowa Sun Dance doll, and of the Cheyenne sacred arrows and medicine hat.[50]

Religiohistorical reconstructions are essential because religion is a product of tradition, and religious data can only be grasped in their historical framing. Religious culture embodies, in a sense, the traces of past religious developments. Radin introduced an approach that has been rather overlooked but still is rewarding in this connection: "reconstruction from internal evidence."[51] The makeup of a culture or a religion, or parts of it, conveys significant information about religious trends in bygone times. The tensions between different patterns in the Plains Shoshoni religion reveal its complex origins.[52]

Particularly rewarding for the Old World history of religions is the documentation of the dissemination of religious traits in North America. Some of these traits join America with Siberia,[53] and others with Europe and the Near East (like the myth of the Earth Diver, the concept of the world tree, the bear cult).[54] Here we encounter world-wide connections which, as a consequence, force us to reevaluate the history of religions even in Southwest Asia. For example, it is not possible any longer to trace religious dualism from Iran when the myth of the divine rival twins is found from the Finns and Slavs to the Lenni Lenape (Delaware) at the North American Atlantic Coast.[55]

The studies of diffusion do more than demonstrate the connections between religious ideas or rituals in the New and Old Worlds. They also tell us that North American religions belong fundamentally to a cultural stratum that may be termed Mesolithic or Late Paleolithic, which stratum constitutes an outgrowth of Arctic culture.[56] The general relations between American and Eurasian religions are thereby defined.

Research on the Structure and Function of Religion

The field studies of North American Indian religions furnish the investigators with a key to the understanding of the interplay between religion on one side and culture, society, and ecology on the other. The field scene is a valuable laboratory where different theories may be tested and different interrelationships investigated. Here again the *point de repère* is religion, and the results are designed to throw light on the structure and function of religion.

North American Indian data are significant for this kind of research for the following reasons: the societies are small and well circumscribed, direct observation is possible in most particulars, and the role of religion is easy to survey. The field analyses of the relations between religion and society are numerous,[57] but most often focus on the contribution religion makes to society, not the other way round. It is characteristic, for instance, that moiety systems are seen as social systems only, whereas to the student of religion they reveal religious functions and, very often, religious motivations. Indeed, as Müller has suggested, even the kinship structure expresses values that govern religious emotions and religious ideals.[58] Here is a new frontier of religious research which has scarcely been opened as yet.

The same judgment applies to the studies of the interactions of religion and ecology. There is a growing understanding among Americanists of the dependence that aboriginal cultures and societies owe to the surrounding nature. By making close analyses of the interplay between religion and nature in the same societies we can stimulate the discussion in the history of religions of the principal import of such relations. It seems that this issue has been almost completely neglected. This is unfortunate, for, basically, the social and cultural ideas that feed religion in technically less-developed cultures are dependent upon environmental factors.

Research on Religious Acculturation

Closely allied with the tasks just referred to are the analyses of syncretism or, as it may also be called, religious acculturation. Through careful observations in the field of present-day religious situations, the student becomes equipped with tools to analyze this specific form of culture contact. Viewed formally, such contact has always taken place, except in isolated marginal societies. Practically speaking, however, it is preferably the modern contact situations that lend themselves to thorough scrutiny. In studying the clash between traditional tribal religion and Christianity among North American Indian groups, we are provided with observations of regularities of religious process that may serve other operational investigations in other parts of the world and at other times. Indeed, we may also be able to formulate some principles of religious process.

The acculturation studies which may be said to have started with Mooney's famous paper on the Ghost Dance (1896) have been coming since the 1930s when their theoretical importance was first appreciated. By now there is vast literature on religious acculturation in North America.[59] In this regard the following topics may be singled out as being particularly significant for the history of religions:

1. Research on prophetic and messianic movements, mainly the Ghost Dance and associated cults (the Plateau Prophet Dance, Puget Sound Shakerism). Most of these movements now belong to the past. Recently Jorgensen has ranged the Plains Sun Dance among them.[60]

2. Research on other new, mixed religions, such as the partly aboriginal, partly Christian Peyote Cult.[61]

3. Research on the progressive history of syncretism in particular

tribal societies. Works in this field include thematic studies like Walker's paper on Nez Perce religious acculturation which registers the influence of factionalism, sects, and political parties on religious development.[62]

As mentioned earlier there are also tendencies of contraacculturation, represented by revivalism ("nativism") and persistence of traditional religious patterns.

The studies of religious acculturation in North America are important because they illustrate emergent forms of religion. Weston La Barre has chosen the title *The Ghost Dance* for his provocative work on the origins of religion, wherein North American Indian religion plays a decisive role.[63]

Research on Religious Personalities

It remains to be said that data from Indian North America provide material for the study of religious personalities, medicine men, prophets, and cult leaders. Fifty years ago, Radin's monograph on a Winnebago creative individual formed a new genre of religioethnographical literature, and names like "Crashing Thunder," "Gregorio the Hand-Trembler" and "Black Elk" are imprinted forever in the treasury of religious autobiographies.[64] They show, most convincingly, that grappling with theological problems is not unique to "civilized" man. The dogmamakers, as well as the mystics and the doubters of the Old World, all have their counterparts in the New World.

The earlier writers on Amerindian religions often lacked sensitivity and empathy in depriving the aborigines of more subtle religious expressions. The growing concern with the Indian as a human being has brought about a better understanding of him as *homo religiosus*. It is most urgent that those involved in religious research among American Indians evince *Einfühlung*, respect the Sacred, and try to read its meaning. In so doing they enhance the importance of their research as a contribution to the history of religions.

NOTES

1. W. C. Smith, "Comparative Religion: Whither—and Why?" in Mircea Eliade and J. M. Kitagawa, eds., *The History of Religions: Essays in Methodology* (Chicago: Chicago University Press, 1959), pp. 37–38.

2. The term *primitive religion*, when met in this article, should be understood in this sense.

3. It seems less meaningful in religious research to make the condition that the student's results should be accepted by members of the religious community involved. What if they demand that the researcher should share their particular convictions?

4. See the discussion of "Urgent Anthropology" in *Current Anthropology* 12, no. 2 (1971):243–54.

5. Cf. Å. Hultkrantz, "North American Indian Religion in the History of Research: A General Survey," parts 1–4, *History of Religions* 6, no. 2 (1966), 91–107; 6, no. 3 (1967), 183–207; 7, no. 1 (1967), 13–34; 7, no. 2 (1967), 112–148.

6. R. Pettazzoni, *Miti e leggende*, vol. 3, *America settentrionale* (Torino, 1953), and *The All-Knowing God: Researches into Early Religion and Culture* (London: Methuen & Co., 1956), pp. 354–403.

7. E. O. James, "The Concept of the Soul in North America," *Folk-Lore* 38 (1927):338–57.

8. M. Eliade, *Shamanism: Archaic Techniques of Ecstasy*, Bollingen Series 76 (New York: Pantheon Books, 1964), pp. 288–322.

9. U. Bianchi, *Il Dualismo Religioso* (Rome, 1958), pp. 69–138.

10. J. E. Brown, *The Spiritual Legacy of the American Indian*, Pendle Hill Pamphlet 135 (Wallingford, Pa., 1964), p. 27.

11. Voget, 1948.

12. Dusenberry, 1962.

13. Cf. F. Eggan, "Social Anthropology and the Method of Controlled Comparison," *American Anthropologist* 56, no. 5 (1954):57; Å Hultkrantz, "The Study of North American Indian Religions: Retrospect, Present Trends and Future Tasks," *Temenos* 1 (1965):88; and Hultkrantz, 1965–67, p. 31.

14. J. M. Cooper, "The Gros Ventres of Montana," part 2, in R. Flannery, ed., *Religion and Ritual*, Catholic University of America Anthropological Series no. 16 (Washington, D.C., 1956).

15. M. I. Hilger, *Arappaho Child Life and Its Cultural Background*, Bureau of American Ethnology Bulletin no. 148 (Washington, D.C., 1952).

16. P. J. Powell, *Sweet Medicine: The Continuing Role of the Sacred Arrows, the Sun Dance, and the Sacred Buffalo Hat in Northern Cheyenne History*, 2. vols. (Norman: University of Oklahoma Press, 1969). It is a strange coincidence that all these authors have a professional religious background. People engaged in ecclesiastical work seem at present to be more intrigued by traditional religions than the numerous anthropologists.

17. A. W. Bowers, *Mandan Social and Ceremonial Organization* (Chicago: University of Chicago Press, 1950), and A. W. Bowers, *Hidatsa Social and Ceremonial Organization*, Bureau of American Ethnology Bulletin no. 194 (Washington, D.C., 1965).

18. G. Catlin, *O-kee-pa: A Religious Ceremony and other Customs of the Mandans*, edited by J. C. Ewers (New Haven and London: Yale University Press, 1967).

19. J. E. Brown, *The Sacred Pipe: Black Elk's Account of the Seven Rites of the Oglala Sioux* (Norman: University of Oklahoma Press, 1953).

20. It would be a great service to the study of religion if the valuable manuscripts on Dakota religion prepared or inspired by Deloria, Bushotter, and other Dakota Indians could be published.

21. W. Müller, *Glauben und Denken der Sioux: Zur Gestalt archaischer Weltbilder* (Berlin: Dietrich Reimer, 1970).

22. J. C. Ewers, *Indian Life on the Upper Missouri* (Norman: University of Oklahoma Press, 1968), pp. 131–145.

23. L. Dräger, "Einige indianische Darstellungen des Sonnentanzes aus dem Museum für Völkerkunde in Leipzig," *Jahrbuch des Museums für Völkerkunde zu Leipzig* 18 (Berlin, 1961):59–86.

24. H. Hartmann, "Die Gros Ventres und ihr Hochgott," *Zeitschrift für Ethnologie* 93, no. 1–2 (Braunschweig, 1968):73–83.

25. Å. Hultkrantz, "Prairie and Plains Indians," *Iconography of Religions* 10, no. 3 (Leiden, 1973).

26. G. L. Coale, "Notes on the Guardian Spirit Concept among the Nez Perce," *Internationales Archiv für Ethnographie* 43 (1958):135–45.

27. E. Arbman, *Ecstasy or Religious Trance*, vol. 2 (Stockholm: Svenska Bokförlaget, 1968), pp. 573–605.

28. P. Albers and S. Parker, "The Plains Vision Experience: A Study of Power and Privilege," *Southwestern Journal of Anthropology* 27, no. 3 (1971):203–33.

29. Å. Hultkrantz, "Spirit Lodge, a North American Shamanistic Seance," in C. M. Edsman, ed., *Studies in Shamanism*, vol. 1 (Uppsala: Scripta Instituti Donneriani Aboensis, 1967), and C. E. Schaeffer, *Blackfoot Shaking Tent*, Occasional Paper no. 5 (Calgary, Alberta: Glenbow-Alberta Institute, 1969).

30. W. Lindig, Geheimbünde and Männerbünde der Prärie- und der Valdland-indianer Nordamerikas, *Studien zur Kulturkunde*, vol. 25, (Wiesbaden: Franz Steiner Verlag, 1970).

31. Å. Hultkrantz, "The Structure of Theistic Beliefs among North American Plains Indians," *Temenos* 7 (1971):66–74.

32. C. L. Smithson and R. C. Euler, *Havasupai Religion and Mythology,* Anthropological Papers of Utah University no. 68 (Salt Lake City, 1964).

33. F. Boas, *Kwakiutl Ethnography*, edited by H. Codere (Chicago and London: University of Chicago Press, 1966).

34. See the works by H. Hickerson, "Notes on the Post-Contact Origin of the

Midewiwin," *Ethnohistory* 9, no. 4 (1962):404–23; H. Hickerson, "The Sociohistorical Significance of Two Chippewa Ceremonials," *American Anthropologist* 65, no. 1 (1963):67–85; W. Muller, Die blaue Hutte: Zum Sinnbild er Perle bei nordamerikanischen Indianern, *Studien zur Kulterkunde*, vol. 12 (Wiesbaden, 1954): A. Dorsinfang-Smets, La Recherche du salut chez les Indiens d'Amerique, in *Religions de salut, Annales du Centre d'Etude des Religions*, vol. 2, pp. 113–25 (Bruxelles, 1962); and J.-L. Michon, "La Grande Medicina degli Ojibwa," *Conoscenza Religiosa* 2 (Firenze,/1970): 177–246. Cf. *also* Ruth Landes, *Objiwa Religion and the Midewiwin* (Milwaukee and London: University of Wisconsin Press, 1968).

35. H. H. Penner, "The Poverty of Functionalism," *History of Religions*, 11, no. 1 (1971):91–97. Cf. *also* M. E. Spiro, "Religion: Problems of Definition and Explanation," in M. Banton, ed., *Anthropological Approaches to the Study of Religion*, A. S. A. Monograph no. 3 (London: Tavistock Publications, 1966).

36. Cf. C. W. von Sydow, *Selected Papers on Folklore* (Copenhagen: Rosenkilde and Bagger, 1948), pp. 147–48, 151–53, 163–65; and B. Ankermann, "Die Religion der Naturvolker," in A. Bartholet and E. Lehmann, eds., *Chantepie de la Saussaye's Lehrbuch der Religionsgeschichte*, 4th ed., vol. 1 (Tubingen: Verlag J. C. B. Mohr, 1925), p. 172.

37. G. Widengren, *Religionens ursprung*, 2nd ed. (Stockholm: Aldus/Bonniers, 1963), p. 85.

38. W. Muller, "Die Pawnee in Nebraska: Lebensbild eine Naturvolkes," *Antaios* 11, no. 5 (1970):412–39, esp. p. 412.

39. E. M. Loeb, *The Blood Sacrifice Complex*, American Anthropological Association Memoir no. 30 (Menasha, Wisconsin, 1923).

40. A. E. Jensen, *Myth and Cult among Primitive Peoples* (Chicago: University of Chicago Press, 1963), pp. 83–190.

41. Cf. J. E. Brown, "The Unlikely Associates: A Study in Oglala Sioux Magic and Metaphysics," *Ethnos* 35 (1970):5–15, and Å. Hultkrantz, "Attitudes to Animals in Shoshoni Indian Relegion," *Studies in Comparative Religion* 4, no. 2 (Bedfont, Middlesex, 1970):70–79.

42. Å. Hultkrantz, "The Owner of the Animals in the Religion of the North American Indians: Some General Remarks," in Å. Hultkrantz, ed., *The Supernatural Owners of Nature, Stockholm Studies in Comparative Religion*, vol. 1 (Stockholm, 1961), pp. 53–64.

43. H. Findeisen, *Das Tier als Gott, Dämon und Ahne* (Stuttgart: Kosmos, 1956), p. 75.

44. I have elaborated this observation more closely in Å. Hultkrantz, "The Structure of Theistic Beliefs among North American Plains Indians," *Temenos* 7 (1971):66–74.

45. Cf. Å. Hultkrantz, "An Ideological Dichotomy: Myths and Folk Beliefs among the Shoshoni Indians of Wyoming," *History of Religions* 11, no. 4 (1972):339–53.

46. J. H. Howard, *The Southeastern Ceremonial Complex and Its Interpretation*, Missouri Archaeological Society Memoir no. 6 (Columbia, 1968).

47. W. W. Fenton, *The Iroquois Eagle Dance: An Offshoot of the Calumet Dance*, Bureau of American Ethnology Bulletin no. 156 (Washington, D.C., 1953).

48. Cf. R. H. Lowie, *Lowie's Selected Papers in Anthropology*, edited by C. Du Bois (Berkeley and Los Angeles: University of California Press, 1960), pp. 202–210.

49. Cf. R. C. Euler, "Ethnographic Methodology: A Tri-Chronic Study in Culture Change, Informant Reliability, and Validity from the Southern Paiute," in C. L. Riley and W. W. Taylor, eds., *American Historical Anthropology, Essays in Honor of Leslie Spier* (London and Amsterdam: Southern Illinois University Press, 1967).

50. W. S. Nye, *Bad Medicine and Good: Tales of the Kiowas* (Norman: University of Oklahoma Press, 1962), pp. 51–56; and P. J. Powell, *Sweet Medicine.*

51. P. Radin, *The Method and Theory of Ethnology* (New York and London: McGraw Hill, 1933), pp. 183–252.

52. Å. Hultkrantz, "Religion und Mythologie der Prärie-Schoschonen," in *Proceedings of the 34th International Congress of Americanists* (Wien, 1962), pp. 546–54.

53. See the trait list in Å. Hultkrantz, "Type of Religion in the Arctic Hunting Cultures: A Religio-Ecological Approach," in H. Hvarfner, ed., *Hunting and Fishing, Nordic symposium of life in a Traditional Hunting and Fishing Milieu* (Luleå, 1965), pp. 265–318.

54. General information in G. Hatt, "Asiatic Influences in American Folklore," *Det. Kgl. Danske Videnskabernes Selskab, Historisk-Filologiske Meddelelser* 31, no. 6 (Copenhagen, 1949). Later studies by Count, Haekel, Hultkrantz, Müller, Paulson and others strengthen Hatt's arguments and deal with other religious traits as well.

55. E. Count, "The Earth-Diver and the Rival Twins," in S. Tax, ed., *Indian Tribes of Aboriginal America* (Chicago: University of Chicago Press, 1952), pp. 55–62.

56. Cf. W. La Barre, *The Ghost Dance: Origins of Religion* (New York: Doubleday and Co., 1970), pp. 121–160.

57. A sample of titles in Å. Hultkrantz, "The Study of North American Indian Religion: Retrospect, Present Trends and Future Tasks," *Temenos* 1 (1965):87–121, esp. p. 98.

58. Müller, *Glauben und Denken der Sioux*, pp. 162–71.

59. Cf. bibliographic notes in Hultkrantz, "The Study of North American Indian Religion," p. 98 f., 108 ff. See also B. J. Siegel, ed., *Acculturation: Critical Abstracts, North America*, Stanford Anthropological Series no. 2 (Stanford, Calif., 1955).

60. J. G. Jorgensen, *The Sun Dance Religion: Power for the Powerless* (Chicago: University of Chicago Press, 1972).

61. Cf. W. La Barre, "Twenty Years of Peyote Studies," *Current Anthropology* 1, no. 1 (1960):45–60. A recent major work is D. F. Aberle, *The Peyote Religion among the Navaho*, Viking Fund Publications in Anthropology no. 42 (New York, 1966).

62. D. E. Walker, *Conflict and Schism in Nez Perce Acculturation: A Study* of Religion and Politics (Seattle: Washington State University Press, 1968).

63. W. La Barre, *The Ghost Dance: Origins of Religion.*

64. A selection of sources in Hultkrantz, "The Study of North American Indian Religion," p. 99 f.

8

On Approaching
Native American Religions —

A PANEL DISCUSSION

This discussion occurred as part of a symposium of Native American Religions in January, 1973, sponsored by the Institute of Religious Studies, University of California, Santa Barbara. The symposium was prompted by the appointment of Åke Hultkrantz of Stockholm University as Visiting Professor of Religious Studies at UCSB. The panel discussion was video-taped for classroom use. Its contents have been transcribed and edited for inclusion as a chapter within this book.

WALTER CAPPS: We are talking about the development of interest in native American religions. I want to begin this discussion by asking Professor Hultkrantz, who is a native of Sweden, how his interest in American Indians developed.

ÅKE HULTKRANTZ: My interest in American Indians arose at the time of my childhood, when I read all available books about Indians and the novels on the Indian adventures in the past. But the crucial question here is, how can a European become interested in American Indian Religion? It seems a bit farfetched, but actually it is not. In the past, the study of religion in Europe, and particularly in Scandinavia, has been concentrated on the known religions of the more advanced civilizations of the near East, of India, and of the

Far East. From a historical point of view it is most important to study these religions. However, if we want to know the essence of religions and their phenomenology, it is necessary for us to direct our interest also to other religious traditions. I think that the American Indian traditions are particularly important. Finally, American Indian religion is something quite unique in itself, and secondly, it sheds light on other religions. To me it was an easy choice. Among all the religions outside the common European-Asiatic traditions, the American Indian religions appeal to me most—perhaps because if one looks at them in their stress of religious individuality, in their understanding of the relationships between man and nature and man before the powers, they remind one very much of the old Scandinavian religions as they were some thousand years ago. That is why my interest was directed to the North American Indians, and I have been richly rewarded.

CAPPS: Are there many other European scholars who have developed an interest in American Indian religions?

HULTKRANTZ: Yes, there are. There has been some interest in Austria, and some interest particularly in Germany. In Sweden, we have had a strong tradition in this field. I certainly am not the first to study this subject, for there were scholars working in the field even at the beginning of this century.

CAPPS: You have told us that the scholarly interest in this subject has been going on for some time, and yet it is clear that there is a new and surging interest in the subject at the present time. Professor Brown, how do you account for this? What is responsible for the increasing interest in the religion of the native American?

JOSEPH EPES BROWN: There is no easy answer to this question for, as I see the situation, it involves critical examination of some of the deeply rooted premises and prejudices of our American society. Ever since the earliest encounters of Europeans with Native Americans it was assumed and insisted upon that these indigenous peoples be acculturated into the mainstreams of a society convinced of its own superiority in all possible domains. In spite of these assumptions and attempts of many centuries, and the utilization of all possible means to bring about conformity, it finally has become evident to most of us that large segments, at least, of Indian peoples insist on retaining their own lifeways; further, where these traditions have become lost or eroded, groups are today attempting, with ever increasing determination, to rediscover and to reintegrate into their own native values and cultural forms. This process of conscious re-integration has accelerated in recent years due in large part to the peoples' growing disenchantment with the values and lifeways of the so-called white man's world. Paralleling this native feeling and movement is of course that growing malaise within the non-Indian world itself. We are well aware that not only among the younger students, but also among an increasing number of scientists and leaders of our country, hard questions are being raised about funda-mental premises and orientations of our society. Actually, we are being forced to this reevaluation by the nature and means of modern warfare, by the growing deterioration of our natural environment, and by the accompanying and causally related erosion of real values, sense of identity, and quality of life generally. We therefore see taking place differing yet parallel processes of reevaluation on the part of both the Indian and non-Indian. In this mutual awareness there is the possibility that both peoples will at last attempt to learn from each other; that a real and open dialogue will take place between Indian and non-Indian; that above all the non-Indian will at last listen as he has never done before, to learn from the Indian of those ways by which he has lived for thousands of years with reverence and in harmony with this land on which we now both live. This at least is the hope, as I see it.

CAPPS: You are saying, then, that the interest in the subject is not simply a scholarly interest, but is of a personal social, and cultural kind. Anglos have a need to reevaluate where they are and where they are going. And you are also suggesting that the same interest, this reevaluation, the sense of needing to find new directions, is to be found among American Indians? You mentioned that these are parallel developments.

BROWN: Yes, but I do not see this process altogether as a finding of "new directions," but rather as an exploring of new ways for establishing a revitalized continuity, on the part of both Indian and non-Indian, with our respective heritages, grounded as they are in ancient and well-tried traditions. For these are traditions of timeless validity because they are rooted in, and express, the sacred. In this mutual search, the Indian may be closer to such sacred sources than we are, for their rich and varied traditions are deeply rooted in, indeed find their expression in, aspects of the natural environment of this American land; and then, many of their communities miraculously, and against powerful forces, have never lost contact completely with their traditions and sacred lifeways as generally has happened to us. We therefore stand to learn much from such native Americans if, again, we would be willing to give up many of our prejudices, and be able to listen and thus to learn.

CAPPS: Mr. Toelken, have you found it this way too?

BARRE TOELKEN: I agree very much with what he says. I think that rather than trying to find new directions, native Americans seem to be trying to rediscover the old ones. I think there has always been a great interest in the past among native tribes. The past is where one finds traditional information on how to act, how to respond to certain contexts. Yet, in many cases, the past has been erased, or nearly so. The attempt on the part of many is to find what is left of it, to strengthen it, to redevelop it, to make it meaningful, maybe even to discover reasons for being interested in the past again. But so many of the teachers in the past few generations have claimed that one ought not to be interested; rather, one ought to be ashamed of one's past.

On the part of the whites I think it's a bit different. For them, it is not a matter of rediscovering the past, but of discovering someone else's past and using it for a perspective on their own future.

I see two things involved here. One is almost a spiritual or a patriotic recognition of something valuable among the Indians. Dee Brown, in his introduction to *Bury My Heart at Wounded Knee,* says that one reason for the recent interest is that, in an age that has produced no heroes, we find the American Indian to be a hero. Extending that, I think that what we are seeing is that, for the most part, the native American did exactly what anyone in this country would do if he found tomorrow that we were occupied by, say, for example, China. We might be told that our children would have to go to Chinese schools, and learn the language in order to get on, or to make a success of things. We might have certain pressures placed on our religion, our political groups. But I suspect that most of us, for more than a hundred years, would continue to teach our own language, certainly underground if necessary, to try to retain our religious ideas, moral and political systems, and to try to pass them on as far as we could. If our children defected to the conquerer we would devalue them for that. If our grandchildren learned Chinese to get on in the government, we would disown them if we could. I think that what we have to remember is that many native Americans are living at a time when the conquest of their country is not that distant. It is still within the memory of many, and certainly within their grandfathers' memory. While the Indian may be trying to hang onto things that are left from that conquest, I think that the white, witnessing the country's present involvements, sees a sort of patriotism, the sort of faithfulness to one's roots, that has already been demonstrated by the Indian; and I think he wants to emulate this kind of spiritual awareness of it.

Going hand in hand with that, for whites, is the recognition that our straight-line concept of raw materials leading to products is now a dead end. We have economists like Kenneth Boulding suggesting that instead of straight-line economy we need a circular economy. We need something that rehashes and recycles, not in a physical sense, but in a theoretical sense. We cannot assume inexhaustible raw materials, and we cannot assume that we have room for the products and the waste to pile up. Our own models of how things ought to operate would be under questioning even if we did not know about the Indians.

So I think there are several reasons, both spiritual and scientific, for reexamining our own concept of what is happening, and we have suddenly found that our new ideas align very nicely with the ancient ones from the Indians, and it is a pleasant surprise!

CAPPS: Mr. Sekaquaptewa, can you tell us something about how the Indians themselves respond to this new surge of interest on the part of the nonnative American?

EMORY SEKAQUAPTEWA: I am sure that there are mixed feelings about this on the part of native Americans, and this probably depends on the native's own feelings, and stability in his culture, and this certainly varies from one native American to the other. I think that some of us who are more fortunate than others find that we have more security in our culture. In my case, the Hopi culture, by reason of its geographical isolation, has been able to retain the cultural surrounding and atmosphere to a higher degree than you would find in Indians in New York or other places. So there is obviously a difference which may very well affect the attitude that the native American would take toward the interest on the part of the nonnative Indian about him. I understand Professor Brown and Toelken, and generally I would agree. But I also think that the Indian is slowly coming to appreciate the value of his cultural security as the foundation of the enjoyment of a fuller life.

Prior to this, the governmental attitude, having taken the position of guardian to ward over the Indian, simply intimidated the native American with the notion that he must assimilate in order to survive in the American system. He was indeed intimidated by this, and his goal was then to become like a white man. Suddenly, the tide has turned. My feeling is that it is not because the white man has found something valuable to be gained from the Indian worldview or attitude, for what one does not understand one cannot really put a value on. I think that what is happening here is that the white man's technological methods of controlling the environment have begun to produce results which have become a measure of the quality of life. It is really the white man's own question about the quality of his life which leads him to search for potential alternatives in the Indian way of life.

In the meantime, the Indian attitude, or my own personal attitude, is not one where I would say I do not want to share my cultural attitude with the white man—I welcome the white man to learn about me—but I do not see the feasibility of teaching the white man in the same sense that he has tried to teach me about himself. I think that the Indian does not have a feeling of converting the white man to his way in the positive sense in which the white man has attempted to convert the Indian to his way through the formal school system and other kinds of formal institutional impositions.

CAPPS: Apart from the conversion, in your view, does the white man now come to the Indian with the proper kind of questions? Does the American Indian know what the white man is asking?

SEKAQUAPTEWA: Personally, I think the questions that are being asked are valid questions. But I feel that the white man's temperament is revealed in the very way that he manifests his curiosity, particularly regarding technological development. The white man's attitude is positive and dominating, and he is employing this attitude even now in seeking to understand the Indian. The curiosity continues to be placed in the context of an adversary situation, within which the white man expects to gain an expertise so that he can develop products, and mete out the results as an expert. Of course, the Indian does not look at his life in that fashion.

BROWN: There is a very good point here that with all the best intentions of the white to understand the Indian, there is a barrier—a barrier that is created in part by our background and by the literature of our background, which has often been of a very romantic, sentimental nature. If we want to break through that barrier and really penetrate into the inner world of the Indian, it requires more of us than we at least presently are able to accomplish. It requires a revolution in our thinking, a complete turnabout of our worldview. We cannot do this easily. We can approach it as we do in a scholarly way—and this brings certain positive results—but, there is a point beyond which we cannot go. That world remains your world, that is, the world of the native American. Perhaps that is the way it should be, but I think we should try.

SEKAQUAPTEWA: Yes, I think the scholarly approach is perhaps the one that offers the greatest allowance for trying to understand the Indian, and for appreciating Indian thought. What I have attempted to suggest here is that the white man possesses a habit of thinking pragmatically, which is also consistent with the empirical method, and, thus, which tends to require positive, concrete proof. But, fundamentally, human culture, at least from the Indian point of view, is not something which needs this kind of proof and evidence before it has meaning. It is not in this way that culture comes to have importance to the Indian. It may be that the white man is seeking something too pragmatic and concrete in his attempt to understand the Indian.

CAPPS: We recognize that we place different values on our experience. And we know that American Indians view the world differently from the way the white man views the world. But now, is it a matter of viewing the world differently? Or, are there in fact different worlds?

TOELKEN: That's a difficult question, and I perhaps should not even try to answer it. We certainly see the world as we are programmed to see it, and maybe in fact there are different worlds. Some of my close friends among several tribes have what the whites call mystical experiences—that is, seeing or experiencing something that is "unreal" or from the "other" world. And yet the people who have those experiences generally do not describe them as being otherworldly or unreal. Such experiences are part of this existence.

I think we are also guilty of looking intentionally for different things, and maybe this is something we can cope with. The whites in general—and I do not mean to be derogatory when I say this—have been trained to look at things and at actions. So, for example, when we study naitve American tribes we are likely to look at implements or at dances, or at events that startle or are unique—things that can be photographed, touched, catalogued, or put into the data sheets and submitted to what we call empirical study. I suspect that if many whites went to a family gathering in the middle of the afternoon among Navajos, where people sit for perhaps two or three hours without doing or saying anything, they might conclude that nothing is happening. But I would suggest that maybe the best way to learn about the Indians that I know anything about is not to look at their artifacts, but to sit for three hours and "do nothing" with them. In fact, something is happening, but something other than what we have been trained to watch for. Such "happenings" belong to the field of interrelationships of human beings and interrelations of man with nature; all of this pertains to what we, in our culture, might refer to as abstractions or unprovables. It seems to me that this is where the essence of most native American cultures lies. Therefore, it is very difficult to study since we have been taught to look only for certain things or to ask only for certian names. For example, the basic question that we ask of each other—"What's your name? Who are you?"—cannot be asked of some people among certain tribes. Such persons are not supposed to tell. Some of the most basic information that we feel we need to know is either illogical or taboo in many native American contexts.

I think your earlier question, while almost unanswerable, is really one of the central points of our whole discussion: do we really ask the proper questions in order to find out what we think we are looking for? I guess I am suggesting that we seldom know which questions to ask.

CAPPS: There must be some continuity, since some communication between the two worlds does go on.

TOELKEN: I am not sure why that is the case. I think it is that the Indians are listening more carefully than we are. For a long time, the communication has been almost exclusively one way, with some exceptions. We have learned some medicine, we have learned some politics, we have learned some other things. One historian even suggests that the whole idea of revolution came about because the Europeans discovered Indians with no kings. The earlier idea was that kings were of the nature of things, supplied by God. Though a king might be bad, the idea of kingship was accepted. But when they saw the American Indians living what was thought to be a kind of noble sort of life, a natural life without kings, the argument was raised that if kings are not natural, why not get rid of some of them. Several historians have pointed out that shortly after this discovery events like the American Revolution and the French Revolution followed. And they suggest that the advent of modern political systems can be dated from the discovery of the Indians without kings. Thus, some information has come our way, but as Dan George says, "We wish you had learned more from us." I think it is true that we have tried to teach more than we have tried to learn.

HULTKRANTZ: I must object a little to what you said here, because I do not think that revolutions came about because the American Indians had no kings. Actually, when I was among the Shoshoni Indians, our chief was more like a king than a president, and there was a tendency toward dynastic heritage in that tribe. Furthermore, there are many hereditary chiefs in North America. We even talk about the kingdoms of the Southeastern tribes. Certainly we have the dynasties among the Aztecs and among the Peruvian Indians, and so on. So I need to sound a word of caution.

Now, to me, this discussion is most interesting because it shows that there are two different approaches to the study of American Indian religions. One is a value-dominated approach, which, for the most part, has been documented here. The emphasis on spiritual values in American Indian religions is great, and also the stress on meditation—which I prize very highly—and which is combined in our day with trends coming from the Far East—I am referring to the Asiatic Indian and Far Eastern thinking that has emerged from interest in Buddhism and Hinduism. All that has stimulated the growth of a new interest in meditation in Europe and in America. That stream of influence is cross-fertilized by the stream of influence coming from the North American Indians, and is most healthy. Now this is one inroad for the study of American religions, and it is, perhaps, the most important. But it is also the most difficult one.

The other approach, which has been taken by us who are in Europe, because we have the American Indians at a distance and cannot easily go out to the reservations and see them, is to study what I have called the phenomenology of religions. I consider that it is a must now, among students of religion, to know the American Indian religions. We have not known enough about them. There was interest in this topic some fifty or sixty years ago when American anthropologists published very interesting cases and commentaries to these cases, on Wakanda, Orenda, and Manitou, and so on. But after the 1920s, there has not been a real approach to knowledge of American Indian religions. That knowledge is now coming back to us and becoming part of our general treasure of religious traditions, and I think that is most important. The way in which we can study it, then, is also by pointing out the different forms, the interrelationships between religions and cultures, but continually stressing religion as such, not reducing religion to something else as has been so extremely common in the scientific debate, not least in this country. We must try to see religion for the value it has, while recording at the same time the forms of religion as well as the traditions in which these forms have been passed on.

CAPPS: Professor Hultkrantz, you have done an excellent job of separating things for us and distinguishing things. I hear you saying that the interest in native American religions is at least twofold: on the one hand, it derives from certain spiritual crises in American life; on the other hand, there is an interest in developing the study of American Indian religions among phenomenologists or historians of religion. You are also suggesting that these two strands may not always have the same objectives. Heretofore we have been talking primarily about the spiritual-value approach to the subject. Now on the other side, in terms of phenomenology of religion and history of religion, I know that you have been a champion of the cause that one cannot master phenomenology of religion, even know his way around in it properly, unless he has some thorough acquaintance with North American Indian religions.

HULTKRANTZ: This is correct.

CAPPS: And I would also guess that what you are saying has not been heard around the world. I would like to ask you how far this art has progressed. Is this a newer field than I realize? Are there only a few people involved in it? Are there courses on this subject in the schools for example, not only in the universities, but even at the lower levels of education? Is this happening in your country?

HULTKRANTZ: I have been called upon to teach in high schools as well as other places on this subject.

BROWN: I would like to mention that as a student with Professor Hultkrantz I was impressed with how well they have done their homework in Sweden. On occasion I was asked to talk about American Indian affairs to groups, and I was terrified because on so many points they knew so much more than I did. I found this to be true not only in Sweden, but also in other countries, especially in Germany. I think that this renaissance owes a great deal to what has been fermenting among European scholars. They have had from their distance often a much better perspective as to what has been going on here than we have had.

TOELKEN: I think, too, that the phenomenon is complicated in the United States and in Canada by political factors. In a very real sense most of us here are living on Indian land, and so it is almost a kind of spiritual necessity to play down the importance of the Indian. A great amount of spiritual credence to what goes on in Indian religion, especially since ironically it deals so closely with man and the land, forces us to examine our own existence here more closely, perhaps, than most of us want to. I do not say that this is a conscious idea discussed by people very often. But when I visit areas where there is a large Indian population, even though Indians and whites are living very close geographically, there is almost a complete rejection of each other, an unwillingness to talk, an unwillingness to know what really goes on. Instead of interest in learning to talk to one another, there is the attitude that "well, those people don't amount to much. Why don't *they* just shape up and join *us*." This attitude affects the serious study of Indian religious matters in this country in a way that the Europeans have not experienced.

On the other hand, I must say in fairness, that a good many public schools across the country are beginning to offer courses in native American literature and culture. Although their main interest is not the religious content of these materials (taken from a native American point of view), many of these literary expressions are nonetheless religious in nature, and consequently there is an increasingly greater exposure to these religious ideas in the primary and secondary grades.

CAPPS: What is the motivation for this?

TOELKEN: In schools I have visited it is sometimes a kind of charitable way of saying, "Well, the Indians also had a few interesting things to say. Let's take a look at them." It is almost condescending in some cases. In other cases, I should say that there is a real commitment to it, but often it is for sociological reasons. I have heard teachers say, "We need to give our Indian young people something to study in school, something to help boost their morale." Sometimes this helps. But I find very little real concern about Indian religious values on the part of these teachers. It is as if they are working some new thing into the curriculum in order to help someone out.

For that reason I do not denigrate it, because I think that is as fair a reason as any. But I also suspect that, although these courses are spreading, they cannot be taken as indications of a serious interest in Indian religions. On the other hand, the whole development may indeed cause an *exposure* which can cause a lot of students to become more deeply involved.

CAPPS: With respect to this exposure, what do you say to complete novices in the subject, persons who have little or no background or training, but have a developing interest, and do not know what to do with it, in which direction to push it? What recommendations can you make at that point to further the exposure or to extend the interest?

BROWN: I might mention that at the University of Montana I constantly get letters from universities around the country asking, "Do you have a summer seminar to which teachers can go to learn about these teachings, how to handle the materials, and how to approach the teaching in the native American field?" In Montana we are now in the process of building programs in Indian Studies, and one of the programs that I think is important will be a program for teachers of American Indian studies.

Generally, however, one of the large problems we all have regarding new curricular programs in American Indian studies has to do with the approaches Professor Hultkrantz outlined for us. That is, on the one hand we can draw upon an academic approach; on the other hand there is the more experiential approach, which is the Indian way. It would be wrong for us to design native American programs exclusively according to the canons of standard models of scholarship, and then ask the Indian to come in and to identify with them. This is what we have been doing all along, and I think it is time to stop this. With regard to our relation to the native American, we should have a little more imagination in developing programs which focus on the Indian quality of environment. I do not know how we can do this, but I think we are wrong in any case to set up our own academic program and then ask the Indian to insert himself into it. I see a dual way in which we should be considering the development of programs. For the non-Indian, certainly, the more academic approach is appropriate, but in our relation to the Indian we have to create something new, something else. What it is to be, what forms it should take, I do not know, but I believe we should think about it a great deal.

SEKAQUAPTEWA: I do not have anything in the way of an answer as to how this should be accomplished. I too am seeking the best way to create the kind of exposure that would achieve this transfer of understanding. At the University of Arizona in Tucson we have an American Indian Studies program, which is denominated as an interdisciplinary approach, but it is not one which could come close to the degree of sophistication that we are reaching for in this discussion. We desire a way to help the Indian student and the non-Indian student together to make a mutual adjustment and to work together to improve their relationship. But we really do not have a method of doing this. Instead, we tend to rely on the Indian student to come in and to open himself up for exposure to his non-Indian counterpart. Then we are not the ones who are telling the non-Indian what the Indian culture is, or what his thoughts are. Rather, the Indian himself who becomes involved in the program voluntarily does this. Again, this is not any kind of a deliberate program. We are not doing anything which has set schedules for accomplishment. It is something we have a great interest in, but we have not been able to find answers. My experience has been, as you have said, that many teachers at the elementary and secondary school levels have shown an interest only to the point of wanting to help the child make the adjustment to his non-Indian environment. This is different from helping the child become stronger in himself and in his own cultural environment.

CAPPS: Mr. Toelken?

TOELKEN: In response to the first part of your question about what to tell novices: this poses a puzzle because almost everyone is a novice in someone else's culture. And that goes, too, for native Americans about each other's cultures. Often tribes in the East do not know much about how tribes in the West think. A lot of information needs to be exchanged. I always invite teachers to consult two of Edward T. Hall's books, *The Silent Language* and *The Hidden Dimension*, as fast as they can. Both of these books contain ideas which I disagree with to some extent, but both are useful in showing how different cultures view matters of space and time, and how cultures communicate those matters. If we can get the beginner to recognize how different those matters can be, and then encourage him to make local contacts with the particular group he is interested in learning more about, after he is aware of the relativity of human forms of awareness, it is very likely that he will learn.

To illustrate, there is a difference between Indian time and white time. Indian events normally flower of themselves; Indian time is not arbitrarily set by the clock, and if the white realizes that and goes, say, to an Indian ceremony or to a dance, or simply to visit an Indian family, he is likely to be far more comfortable when silences occur, when time passes, when events come about naturally. But, if he goes having heard that there will be a ceremonial at 7:30, and goes at 7:15 to get a good seat, and sits there and waits, he will be extremely frustrated by the time nine o'clock rolls around and the event has not started yet (many ceremonials may not start till two or three o'clock in the morning). Often, everyone just sits there, Indian style, sort of savoring each other's presence, then, when enough people have come forward to man the drum or to dance, things will get going. If one knows that, he will not be intimidated by it, and he will learn more. At times a lot of us are not aware of how differently various cultures handle those sorts of experiences. It is a very fundamental knowledge. Without that awareness, a mere reading of the most scholarly books in the greatest number will never enable the novice really to know something about another culture.

CAPPS: Professor Hultkrantz, will you comment on the same question?

HULTKRANTZ: It is a crucial question of course. I should like to comment on what Professor Brown talked about. I think that it is possible to establish two ways of approaching the American Indian religions. One way is the one in which particular Indians, the Indians themselves, expose and exhibit their patterns, their values, their traditions, the roles of religion in their culture, etcetera, monographically. By that I mean simply that they handle these traditions within the framework of their own cultures, their own background, as Emory Sekaquaptewa suggested. This is very important. Another way is through a comparative understanding of different traditions; from this set of interests, we attempt to put the puzzle together as well as we can. Of course, comparative work always involves examination of the skeleton of things. As hard as one tries, he can never really penetrate deeply. But he must try to, and then compare the Indian traditions first with each other, and then within the larger context of the religions that we have all over the world. A blending of these two approaches might be a very good way for carrying out cooperation between the Indians themselves and we who are foreigners. Perhaps this way we can come closer to the real significance of the Indian traditions.

CAPPS: Our time is going quickly. But I want to raise another issue, for it plays into the interest we are pursuing right now. If one were to study the genesis of personal interest in American Indians among nonnative Americans, I would suspect he would find that many persons' interest in the subject was first stimulated through exposure to a particular individual, that is, to a living native American. In my own case, for example, it was through listening to my grandfather talk about his contact with Indians in Nebraska and the Dakotas. I went from there to novels and biographies of native American figures. Such, I suspect, has been the pattern for many.

We touched upon this aspect earlier when we referred to the absence of heroes in contemporary American life, and about the consequent turning to American Indian cultures with an interest in finding heroes. If one places this tendency within the context of all that is being said about models of personality formation in our time, say from Robert Jay Lifton's "protean man" to the observations and contentions of Norman O. Brown, we may be in touch with a new way of approaching our subject. Perhaps our interest in native American religions—witness the works of Carlos Castenadas—is motivated by a search for a new or more viable model of personality formation.

I do indeed wish we had more time, for I'd like to ask each of you about this personal dimension. How about your own exposure to native American personalities? What sort of characteristics have you found? What strategies—personal or otherwise—are involved in turning attention that way? How would you distinguish native American personality characteristics from Anglo habits of mind or ways of life? Can they be distinguished? Is this an inappropriate or insensitive question? In what sense can native American personalities be looked to as heroes? Can they really function as models of personality formation? Are they personally accessible?

Professor Brown, will you say something about Black Elk.

BROWN: Well, it is a crucial question. Indeed, my own interest started at a very early age. I grew up in a very tight environment, but had the good fortune to spend a large part of my time at a place in the Maine woods as a child. We had a little cabin by a stream there, and there was nothing much to do. But there was an Indian who used to trap there. As a child of five or six I made friends with him, and we used to spend hours together. He would tell me stories about the animals and about the world, and this was the beginning of a great encounter. One cannot live in close proximity to such a person without absorbing some of the sacredness of the person. I am not sure how to put it—one cannot describe these qualities very well in our own language. I am referring to the presence of a living personality, and this is the deciding influence.*

---

* Professor Brown has had occasion to expand on this subject, with particular reference to Black Elk, in his *The Sacred Pipe* (Norman: University of Oklahoma Press, 1953, published as a Penguin Book, 1971), a portion of which has been reprinted in *The North American Indians*, photographs by

CAPPS: I was afraid of it. Our time is gone. Let me simply thank all of you for participating in the symposium around which this discussion has occurred, and also for contributing to the present discussion. I am certain that this is not the last time we will converse about this subject. I hope we have come some distance toward adding information to the discussion, or, perhaps more exactly, of getting the discussion properly set so that something more can be done about it in the future. I am particularly hopeful that we can make use of some of the suggestions that have been given us regarding curricular design in the proper, sensitive manner, so that both of these approaches—the phenomenology of religion and the concern about personal spirituality—will be respected.

Edward S. Curtis, text and introduction by Joseph Epes Brown (New York: Aperture Books, 1972).

Selected Bibliography

Aberle, David F. *The Peyote Religion Among the Navaho* (Chicago: Aldine, 1966).

Albers, P. and S. Parker. "The Plains Vision Experience: A Study of Power and Privilege," in *Southwestern Journal of Anthropology*. XXVII, 3 (1971), 203–33.

Alexander, Hartley B. *The World's Rim* (Lincoln: University of Nebraska Press, 1967).

Artaud, Antonin. *The Peyote Dance* (New York: Farrar, Strauss and Giroux, 1976).

Ashe, Geoffrey. *Land to the West* (New York: Viking Press, 1962).

Bailey, Paul. *Ghost Dance Messiah* (Los Angeles: Westernlore Press, 1970).

Benedict, Ruth. "The Vision in Plains Culture," in *American Anthropologist*. XXIV (1922), 1–23.

———. *The Concept of the Guardian Spirit in North America*. Memoirs of the American Anthropological Association, No. 29 (1923).

Boas, Franz. *Kwakiutl Ethnography*, edited by H. Codere (Chicago: University of Chicago Press, 1966).

Bowers, A. W. *Mandan Social and Ceremonial Organization* (Chicago: University of Chicago Press, 1950).

———. *Hidatsa Social and Ceremonial Organization*. Bureau of American Ethnology, Bulletin 194, Washington (1965).

Brown, Dee. *Bury My Heart at Wounded Knee* (New York: Bantam Books, 1972).

Brown, Joseph Epes. *The Sacred Pipe. Black Elk's Account of the Seven Rites of the Oglala Sioux* (Norman: University of Oklahoma Press, 1953).

———. *The Spiritual Legacy of the American Indian* (Wallingford, Pa.: Pendle Hill Pamphlet 135, 1964).

———. "The Unlikely Associates. A Study in Oglala Sioux Magic and Metaphysic," in *Ethnos*. XXXV (1970), 5–15.

Brown, Vinson. *Voices of Earth and Sky. The Vision Life of the Native Americans and their Culture Heroes* (Harrisburg: Stackpole Books, 1974).

Burland, Cottie A. *North American Indian Mythology* (London: Hamlyn, 1966).

Bunzel, Ruth L. "Introduction to Zuni Ceremonialism," *47th Annual Report of the Bureau of American Ethnology*, 1929–30, 467–544.

Catlin, G. *O-kee-pa: A Religious Ceremony and other Customs of the Mandans*, edited by J. C. Ewers (New Haven: Yale University Press, 1967).

Coale, G. L. "Notes on the Guardian Spirit Concept among the Nez Perce," in *Internationales Archiv für Ethnographie*. XLVIII (1958), 135–48.

Covarrubias, Miguel. *The Eagle, the Jaguar, and the Serpent. Indian Art of the Americas* (New York: Alfred A. Knopf, 1954).

E. Count. "The Earth-Diver and the Rival Twins," in S. Tax, editor, *Indian Tribes of Aboriginal America* (Chicago: University of Chicago Press, 1952).

Cronyn, George W. *American Indian Poetry* (New York: Live Right Publishing Corp., 1962).

Curtis, Edward S. *The North American Indian* (New York: Pierpont Morgan Library, 1906–1930). 20 Vols.

———. *The North American Indians. A Selection of Photographs.* Introduction by Joseph Epes Brown (New York: Aperture, 1972).

Cushing, F. H. "Outlines of Zuni Creation Myths," *13th Annual Report of the Bureau of American Ethnology* (1891–1892), 321–447.

Deloria, Vine, Jr. *Behind the Trail of Broken Treatises* (New York: Delacorte Press, 1974).

———. *Custer Died for Your Sins* (New York: Macmillan, 1969).

———. "Religion and Revolution among American Indians," in *Worship* (January, 1974), 12 ff.

———. "The Theological Dimension of the Indian Protest Movement," in *Christian Century* (September 19, 1973), 912 ff.

Densmore, Frances. "*Teton* Sioux Music" *61st Bulletin of the Bureau of American Ethnology* (Washington: Government Printing Office, 1918).

Devereaux, G. *Mohave Ethnopsychiatry* (Washington: Smithsonian Institute, 1961).

Divine, David. *The Opening of the World* (New York: C. P. Putnam's Sons, 1973).

Dockstader, Frederick J. *Indian Art in America* (Greenwich, Conn.: New York Graphic Society, 1961).

Dorsey, George A. *Traditions of the Skidi Pawnee.* Memoirs of the American Folklore Society, VIII (1904).

Eggan, F. "Social Anthropology and the Method of Controlled Comparison," in *American Anthropologist*. LVI, 5 (1954), 743–63.

Eliade, Mircea. *Patterns in Comparative Religion* (New York: Sheed and Ward, 1958).

———. *Shamanism. Archaic Techniques of Ecstasy* (New York: Pantheon Books, Bollingen Series LXXVI, 1964).

Ellis, Richard N. *The Western American Indian: Case Studies in Tribal History* (Lincoln: University of Nebraska Press, 1972).

Erikson, Erik H. *Childhood and Society* (New York: W. W. Norton, 1950), Part Two, 109–86.

Ewers, J. C. *Indian Life on the Upper Missouri* (Norman: University of Oklahoma Press, 1968).

Feldmann, Susan. *The Story Telling Stone* (New York: Dell Publishers, 1971).

Fenton, W. N. *The Iroquois Eagle Dance. An Offshoot of the Calumet Dance* (Washington: Bureau of American Ethnology, 1953).

Fiedler, Leslie A. *The Return of the Vanishing American* (New York: Stein and Day, 1969).

Forman, James. *People of the Dream* (New York: Dell Publishers, 1972).

Fox, J. R. "Religions of Illiterate People: North America," in *Historia Religionum. Handbook for the History of Religions*, edited by C. J. Bleeker and Geo Widengren. Vol. II, *Religions of the Present* (Leiden: E. J. Brill, 1971), 593–608.

Grinnill, George B. *Pawnee Hero Stories and Folktales* (New York: Scribner's, 1912).

Hall, Edward T. *The Hidden Dimension* (Garden City: Doubleday, 1966).

———. *The Silent Language* (Garden City: Doubleday, 1959).

Hallowell, Alfred I. *Culture and Experience* (New York: Schocken Books, 1967).

Harrod, Howard L. *Mission Among the Blackfeet* (Norman: University of Oklahoma Press, 1973).

Heizer, Robert F. and M. A. Whipple. *The California Indians. A Source Book* (Berkeley: University of California Press, 1971).

Hickerson, H. "The Sociohistorical Significance of Two Chippewa Ceremonials," in *American Anthropologist.* LXV, 1 (1963), 67–85.

Howard, J. H. *The Southeastern Ceremonial Complex and Its Interpretation* (Columbia: Missouri Archaeological Society, Memoir 6, 1968).

Holm, Bill. *Crooked Beak of Heaven: Masks and Other Ceremonial Art of the Northwest Coast* (Seattle: University of Washington Press, 1968).

Hultkrantz, Åke. "Anthropological Approaches to Religion," in *History of Religions.* IX, 4 (1970), 337–52.

———. "Attitudes to Animals in Shoshoni Indian Religion," in *Studies in Comparative Religion.* IV, 2 (1970), 70–79.

———. Hultkrantz, Åke. *Conceptions of the Soul Among North American Indians. A Study in Religious Ethnology* (Stockholm: Ethnographical Museum of Sweden, 1953).

———. "An Ideological Dichotomy. Myths and Folk Beliefs Among the Shoshoni Indians of Wyoming," in *History of Religions.* XI, 4 (1972), 339–53.

———. *The North American Indian Orpheus Tradition. A Contribution to Comparative Religion* (Stockholm: Ethnographical Museum of Sweden, 1957).

———. "North American Indian Religion in the History of Research: A General Survey," in *History of Religions.* VI, 2 (1966), 91–107, VI, 3 (1966), 183–207, VII, 1, (1967), 13–34, and VIII, 2 (1967), 112–148.

———. "The Owner of the Animals in the Religion of the North American Indians: Some General Remarks," in Å. Hultkrantz, ed., *The Supernatural Owners of Nature* (Stockholm: Stockholm Studies in Comparative Religion, Vol. I, 1961).

———. "Prairie and Plains Indians," in *Iconography of Religions.* X, 3 (1973).

———. "The Structure of Theistic Beliefs among North American Plains Indians," in *Temenos.* VII (1971), 66–74.

————. "The Study of North American Indian Religions: Retrospect, Present Trends and Future Tasks," in *Temenos*. I (1965), 87–98.

Hungry Wolf, Adolf. *Charlo's People* (Alberta: Good Medicine Books, 1974).

————. *Good Medicine in Glacier National Park* (Alberta: Good Medicine Books, 1971).

————. *Good Medicine Thoughts* (Alberta: Good Medicine Books, 1972).

Hurdy, John M. *American Indian Religions* (Los Angeles: Sherbourne Press, 1970).

James, E. O. "The Concept of Soul in North America," in *Folk-lore*. XXXXVIII (1927), 338–57.

Jensen, A. E. *Myth and Cult Among Primitive Peoples* (Chicago: University of Chicago Press, 1963).

Jorgensen, Joseph G. *The Sun Dance Religion. Power for the Powerless* (Chicago: University of Chicago Press, 1972).

Keiser, Albert. *The Indian in American Literature* (New York: Oxford University Press, 1933).

Krickeberg, Walter, and Hermann Trimborn, Werner Muller and Otto Zerries, *Pre-Columbian American Religions* (New York: Holt, Rinehart and Winston, 1969), 147–229.

Kroeber, Alfred L. "Indian Myths of South Central California," in *University of California Publications in American Archaeology and Ethnology*. IV (1907), 167–250.

———— and E. W. Gifford. "World Renewal: A Cult System of Native Northwest California," *Anthropological Records of the University of California*. XIII (1949).

————. "Yuki Myths," in *Anthropos*. XXVI (1932), 905–39.

La Barre, Weston. "Twenty Years of Peyote Studies," in *Current Anthropology*. I, 1 (1960), 45–60.

————. *The Ghost Dance. Origins of Religion* (Garden City: Doubleday, 1970).

Landes, Ruth. *Ojibwa Religion and the Midewiwin* (Madison: University of Wisconsin Press, 1968).

Lowie, Robert H. *Lowie's Selected Papers in Anthropology*. C. Du Bois, ed (Berkeley: University of California Press, 1960).

————. *Minor Ceremonies of the Crow Indians* (New York: American Museum Press, 1924).

————. *The Religion of the Crow Indians*. Anthropological Papers of the American Museum of Natural History, XXV, Part 2 (1922).

Momaday, N. Scott. *House Made of Dawn* (New York: New American Library, 1968).

————. *The Way to Rainy Mountain* (New York: Ballantine Books, 1969).

Mooney, James. "The Ghost-Dance Religion and the Sioux Outbreak of 1890," *14th Annual Report of the Bureau of American Ethnology*, Part 2 (1896).

Moquin, Wayne, Ed. *Great Documents in American Indian History* (New York: Praeger Publications, 1973).

Muller, Werner. "The 'Passivity' of Language and the Experience of Nature:

A Study in the Structure of the Primitive Mind," in Joseph M. Kitagawa and Charles H. Long, *Myths and Symbols. Studies in Honor of Mircea Eliade* (Chicago: University of Chicago Press, 1969).

Nash, Roderick. *Wilderness and the American Mind* (New Haven: Yale University Press, 1967).

Neihardt, John G. *Black Elk Speaks* (Lincoln: University of Nebraska Press, 1961).

———. *A Cycle of the West* (Lincoln: University of Nebraska Press, 1963).

Nye, W. S. *Bad Medicine and Good. Tales of the Kiowas* (Norman: University of Oklahoma Press, 1962).

Ortiz, Alfonso. *The Tewa World. Space, Time and Becoming in a Pueblo Society* (Chicago: University of Chicago Press, 1972).

Park, Willard Z. *Shamanism in Western North America* (Evanston: Northwestern University Press, 1938).

Parker, A. C. "Secret Medicine Societies of the Seneca," in *American Anthropologist.* N.S. XI (1909), 161–85.

Parsons, E. C. "Crow-Wing. A Pueblo Indian Journal," *Memoirs of American Anthropological Association.* XXXII (1935).

———. *Pueblo Indian Religion,* 2 vols. (Chicago: University of Chicago Press, 1939).

Petrullo, Vincenzo. *The Diabolic Root. A Study of Peyotism* (New York: Octagon Books, 1975).

Powell, P. J. *Sweet Medicine. The Continuing Role of the Sacred Arrows, the Sun Dance, and the Sacred Buffalo Hat in Northern Cheyenne History.* 2 vols. (Norman: University of Oklahoma Press, 1969).

Radin, Paul. *Crashing Thunder. The Autobiography of an American Indian* (New York: Appleton and Company, 1926).

———. *Primitive Religion* (New York: Viking Press, 1937).

———. *The Trickster. A Study in American Indian Mythology* (New York: Schocken Books, 1972).

Reichard, G. A. *Navaho Religion. A Study of Symbolism* (Bollingen Foundation Series XVIII, 1963).

Relander, Click. *Drummers and Dreamers. The Story of Smowhala the Prophet and his Nephew Puck Hugh Toot, the Lost Prophet of the Nearly Extinct River People, the Lost Wanapums* (Caldwell, Idaho: Caxton Printers, 1956).

Ricketts, Mac Linscott. (Review) "J. G. Jorgensen, *The Sun Dance Religion*," in *Journal of the American Academy of Religion.* XLI, 2 (1973), 256–59.

———. *The Structure and Religious Significance of the Trickster-Transformer-Culture Hero in the Mythology of the North American Indians.* University of Chicago Thesis, 1964.

Robbins, William J. "Some Aspects of Pueblo Indian Religion," in *Harvard Theological Review.* XXXIV, 1 (1941), 25–48.

Schaeffer, C. E. *Blackfoot Shaking Tent* (Calgary, Alberta: Glenbow-Alberta Institute Occasional Paper No. 5, 1969).

Schuon, Frithjof. "The Shamanism of the Red Indians." *Light on the Ancient Worlds* (London: Perennial Books, 1965).

Spier, Leslie. "The Sun Dance of the Plains Indians. Its Development and Diffusion," *Anthropological Papers of the American Museum of Natural History*. XVI, Part 7 (1921).

Spinden, Herbert J. *Songs of the Tewa* (New York: Exposition of Indian Tribal Arts, 1933).

Standing Bear, Luther. *Land of the Spotted Eagle* (Boston: Houghton, Mifflin, 1933).

Steiger, Brad. *Medicine Talk. A Guide to Walking in Balance and Surviving on the Mother Earth* (Garden City: Doubleday, 1975).

Steiner, Stan. *The New Indians* (New York: Harper and Row, 1968).

Tedlock, Dennis, ed. *Teachings from the American Earth* (New York: Liveright, 1975).

Teit, James Alexander. *Mythology of the Thompson Indians* (Leiden: E. J. Brill, 1972).

Thompson, Stith. *Tales of the North American Indians* (Bloomington: Indiana University Press, 1966).

Toelken, Barre. "A Circular World: The Vision of Navaho Crafts," in *Parabola*. I, 1 (1975), 30–37.

———."Ma'i Joldloshi. Legendary Styles and Navaho Myth," in *American Folk Legend*, ed. Wayland Hand (Berkeley: University of California Press, 1971), 203–11.

———. "The 'Pretty Languages' of Yellowman. Genre, Mode, and Texture in Navaho Coyote Narratives," in *Folklore Genres*, ed. Dan Ben-Amos (Austin: University of Texas Press, 1976), 145–70.

Underhill, Ruth M. *Ceremonial Patterns in the Greater Southwest* (New York: J. J. Augustin, 1948).

———. *Red Man's Religion* (Chicago: University of Chicago Press, 1965).

Villasenor, David V. *Tapestries in Sand. The Spirit of Indian Sandpainting* (Healdsburg, California: Nature-Graph Company, 1966).

Walker, D. E. *Conflict and Schism in Nez Perce Acculturation. A Study of Religion and Politics* (Seattle: Washington State University Press, 1968).

Waters, Frank. *The Book of the Hopi* (New York: Viking Press, 1963).

———. *Masked Gods. Navaho and Pueblo Ceremonialism* (Denver: Sage Books, 1962).

Wax, Murray L. *Indian Americans. Unity and Diversity* (Englewood Cliffs: Prentice-Hall, 1971).

Wissler, Clark. Ceremonial Bundles of the Blackfoot Indians. *Anthropological Papers of the American Museum of Natural History*. VII, 2 (1912).

———. *Red Man Reservations* (New York: Macmillan, 1971).